1978

SURVIVAL
IN
SPACE

SURVIVAL IN SPACE

By
YURI GAGARIN
and
VLADIMIR LEBEDEV

Translated from the Russian
by Gabriella Azrael

FREDERICK A. PRAEGER, *Publishers*
New York • Washington

BOOKS THAT MATTER

Published in the United States of America in 1969
by Frederick A. Praeger, Inc., Publishers
111 Fourth Avenue, New York, N.Y. 10003

Library of Congress Catalog Card Number: 74–83336

Printed in the United States of America

CONTENTS

SOVIET SPACE FLIGHTS

Craft Name	Date	Astronaut
Vostok-1	April 12, 1961	Yuri Gagarin
Vostok-2	August 6–7, 1961	Gherman Titov
Vostok-3	August 11–15, 1962	Andrian Nikolaev
Vostok-4	August 12–15, 1962	Pavel Popovich
Vostok-5	June 14–19, 1963	Valerii Bykovskii
Vostok-6	June 16–19, 1963	Valentina Tereshkova
Voskhod-1	October 12–13, 1964	Konstantin Feoktistov Boris Egorov Vladimir Komarov
Voskhod-2	March 18–19, 1965	Pavel Belyaev Aleksei Leonov
Soyuz-1	April 23, 1967	Vladimir Komarov
Soyuz-2	October 1968	unmanned
Soyuz-3	October 1968	Georgii Beregovoi
Soyuz-4 and -5 (linkup)	January 18, 1969	Vladimir Shatalov Evgenii Khrunov Aleksei Eliseev Boris Volynov

SURVIVAL
IN
SPACE

CHAPTER ONE

First Flights in Space

Around 100,000 years ago a glacier began to move across Europe bringing with it a sharp drop in temperature. Accustomed to a warm climate, the animals either perished or moved south. Prehistoric man took refuge in caves in his effort to escape the cold. With this natural dwelling, and fire and tools, he managed to adapt to the new way of life.

Hundreds of centuries passed. Great changes took place on Earth. Man's way of life changed. Today his stone or concrete dwelling can be relied on to protect him from the cold of winter and the heat of summer, from rain and bad weather. Artificial heat, light, and air conditioning maintain the most favorable climatic conditions in the home at all times. In this sense it is fair to say with the English that "a man's house is his castle."

But if this castle is fine on Earth, what must the castle be in space, where there is no air, where the temperature varies from $-270°$ C to several thousand degrees above zero F, where space is "shot through" with rays of energy, where meteorites and other heavenly bodies move with great speed?

The first spaceship, Vostok-1, consisted of two basic parts: the hermetically sealed capsule (the descent apparatus) and the propulsion module which contained fuel cells, the propulsion system, the radio equipment, in short, everything necessary for an orbital flight. At the point where the capsule was connected to the propulsion module, there were cylinders of compressed air and pure oxygen to "feed" the cosmonaut's space suit should the cabin suddenly depressurize. On the outside of the propulsion module there was a block of solar cells and a row of antennas for radio transmission.

During the orbit the capsule and the propulsion module were a single whole. For the descent they separated, with the propulsion module condemned to burn out in the atmosphere while the capsule returned to Earth by means of a parachute system. To prevent them from meeting the same fate as the propulsion module, the parachutes were covered with a heat-protective coating. The temperature of the air around a spacecraft reentering the atmosphere is 18,000° F.

The cosmonaut's "cabin" little resembled a home. In the first place it was round, and its living space had to be measured not in square but in cubic feet. The cabin sphere was 7 feet in diameter and 225 cubic feet in total volume.

The appointments consisted of a single chair in which the cosmonaut not only worked but rested and ate. The chair held equipment for the ventilation of the space suit and was shaped to ease acceleration stress when the spacecraft went in or out of orbit. Although it looked like any seat on a cross-country bus or airplane, it was actually a unique flying device, with its own jet engine enabling the cosmonaut to fly out of the capsule and descend to Earth independently by means of a complicated parachute system.

At an altitude of 22,500 feet the hatch flew off automatically, and two seconds later the cosmonaut and his chair were catapulted out. The chair's drogue parachute opened immediately. At an altitude of 13,000 feet it transferred its function to the main parachute which then separated the cosmonaut from the chair and took him back to Earth. As he descended, the radio in the main chute signaled the rescue team. Should the main chute suddenly fail, the cosmonaut had an emergency chute to separate him from his chair and take him down to Earth.

The capsules on the six Vostok flights came down independently with their own parachute systems. At an altitude of 13,000 feet the top of the parachute canister shot off releasing the deployment parachute and the drogue chute. At an altitude of 8000 feet the drogue chute deployed the main chute. The capsule's descent was slow to enable the cosmonaut to return safely to Earth, if that was where he chose to land.

Gherman Titov has said of his experience:

> When Vostok-2 had descended far enough for the catapult I felt a jolt and flew out of the cabin. I was blinded by the bright sun. Over my head the bright orange dome of the chute opened.
>
> Beneath me cumulus clouds were swirling. I went through their density and saw the Earth covered with golden stubble. I recognized the Volga and two towns along its banks, Saratov and Engels. That meant that everything was going as it was supposed to. The landing was going to be right in the target area.
>
> The sunlight came clean and radiant through the clouds as if from under a lampshade. Swaying a bit, the chute floated me farther and farther down.

Aside from the chair the Vostok capsules were equipped with air-purification systems, part of the radio equipment, food, and windows from which one could observe everything taking place on Earth and in space. To Yuri Gagarin, the first man lucky enough to look at Earth from outer space, it felt like this:

> The Earth through the window of the spacecraft looked approximately as it does from a jet plane at high altitudes. The mountain ridges, the great rivers, massive forests, ocean shorelines stood out sharply. I could see both clouds and their faint shadows on the surface of the Earth.
>
> When I looked toward the horizon I saw an unusual distortion very distinctly. The Earth was ringed by a light blue halo, which gradually darkened, turned turquoise, dark blue violet, then coal black.
>
> Trembling with excitement I watched a world so new and unknown to me, trying to see and remember everything. Astonishingly bright cold stars could

be seen through the windows. They were still far away—oh, how far away—but in orbit they seemed closer than the Earth. But the point was not the distance (my distance from the Earth was but a drop in the ocean compared to the light-years separating us from the stars) but the principle. Man had overcome the force of Earth's gravity and gone out into space.

The windows were made of fireproof glass. It was possible to see through them even when the capsule was enveloped in flames at the end of my space flight when the craft went out of orbit and reentered the dense strata of atmosphere. Through the blinds covering the windows I saw the terrible crimson flame raging around the craft. Although inside the cabin it was only 68° F, I was in a cloud of fire rushing toward Earth.

Special venetian blinds protected my eyes from the direct sunlight. I had to use the blinds every time the Sun even peeped in the window. In outer space it shines blindingly bright, probably dozens of times brighter than on Earth.

If you measure Vostok's cabin against a room on Earth, it is quite tiny. But if you compare it to airplane cabins or to the capsules of American space ships, it becomes much more spacious, even comfortable. Valerii Bykovskii, lying in that "room" for the five days of his flight, gave it very high marks. According to the engineers' calculations, it would have been possible to stay in orbit 12 days.

The Vostok was designed for a short flight with one man on board. But the multiseated spaceships designed for long orbits and interplanetary flights will have separate places not only for work and rest, but for other things, for a hothouse, let's say, filled with plants.

Tsiolkovskii's hothouse

To begin with, some history.

On July 18, 1803, two men ascended in a balloon to

an altitude of 23,500 feet. Here is how one of them described his sensations: "We experienced extreme lethargy and some fear as we did our various experiments. The noise in our ears that had started early on kept increasing as the barometer dropped. Our lethargy was somewhat like the sensation a man has when he dives into the water for a swim. ... My pulse was rapid, Lost's slow. ... We were in such a state of moral and physical apathy that we could hardly fight off sleep."

In 1875 three French balloonists in the balloon Zenith attained an altitude of more than 26,000 feet. Not knowing how to use their small quantity of oxygen, two of the team perished. The survivor, the pilot Tisaude, told later of what had happened in the basket. He saw his friends "falling asleep" without making the slightest effort to save themselves. He himself experienced a strange apathy: "At an altitude of 24,000 feet one's condition becomes abnormal, the mind and body gradually and imperceptibly weaken. There is no suffering. On the contrary, one experiences an inner joy, overflowing radiance. One becomes indifferent to everything, you think neither about the danger nor about your own desperate situation."

The tragic events of the flight drew the attention of many investigators. As in the Robertson case, it was obvious that there had been oxygen starvation. So the question arose of how to supply balloonists with the necessary oxygen. In creating the microclimate in the cabin of a spaceship, special attention had to be paid again to this problem.

A normal composition of air on Vostok was supplied by a recirculating system using highly active chemical compounds, which were able to supply the necessary oxygen and at the same time absorb exhaled carbon dioxide, various other harmful gas products formed in the process of human activity, and moisture. Humidity is one of the most important life conditions in the cabin of the spaceship. The most

favorable humidity range in the cabin is from 30%
to 70% and Vostok's recirculating system kept it
within that range.

A molecular sieve was used to absorb the water
vapor saturating the atmosphere in the cabin and,
depending on the amount of vapor and amount of
time involved, either drive it into selected absorbents
in a crystalline form or into a reduction solution. Normal temperature in the cabin was maintained by a
special heat exchanger which released excess heat
into outer space.

Once such chemical compounds have done their
work, they lose their ability to cleanse the air, which
means that the longer the flight, the more recirculating compounds will have to be taken. On an interplanetary flight every gram will count. What is the
solution?

Almost 200 years ago the Swedish chemist K. W.
Scheele discovered oxygen. The English chemist
Joseph Priestley discovered the same gas independently. What Priestley wanted to know was how any
oxygen remains in the atmosphere if it is constantly
being used up in respiration and fire.

In 1771 he was able to prove that animals exhale
air unfit for respiration, but that plants then "clean"
it. He put a mouse under a bell glass on a sunlit win-
dowsill and after several hours the mouse died for
lack of oxygen. But when he put a sprig of mint in
with a mouse the animal behaved normally and
suffered no discomfort whatever. Although Priestley's
discovery greatly impressed his contemporaries it soon
became clear that the experiment would not always
work.

In 1779 the Dutch scientist Jan Ingenhousz added
a substantial qualification: he proved that green
plants "clean" the air only in the Sun. Then in 1782
the Swiss botanist Jean Senebe definitively established that plants absorb carbon dioxide from the air
and turn it back into oxygen and carbon. The oxygen

is released into the atmosphere while the carbon, with water, is turned into hydrocarbons—carbohydrates (sugar, starch). This process is called photosynthesis.

K. A. Timiryazev showed that photosynthesis can take place only in the sunlight and only in the green part of the plant—in the grains of chlorophyll. He also established that these grains do not absorb all the visible rays of the spectrum, only the red and the blue violet.

It was the Earth itself, essentially an enormous spaceship in the vastness of the universe, that suggested the solution to the problem of cleansing the air. Konstantin Tsiolkovskii was the first to see the solution when he proposed that the basic atmospheric purification cycle that takes place on Earth be reproduced in miniature in spaceships. He wrote: "Just as Earth's atmosphere is cleansed by plants with the help of the Sun, so should our artificial atmosphere be able to renew itself, be able to maintain the rotation of the elements necessary for human life—oxygen and water—and to clean the air of carbon dioxide."

Tsiolkovskii's idea only began to be implemented in our day. The first experiments conducted in scientific laboratories showed that there were difficulties behind the apparent simplicity of the idea. In fact the problem was to create an ecological closed system that would replicate all the functions that concern man on the Earth's biosphere.

We will not concern ourselves with the full cycle of the exchange of matter, just with the exchange of gases. On an average day a man uses 2.2 pounds of oxygen and manufactures 2.9 pounds of carbon dioxide. How is the balance between plants and man achieved? How can a hothouse be built in weightlessness? How does one choose the plants and provide for their reproduction? Scientists all over the world are working on these questions.

Chlorella is sometimes called a space plant although it is fully at home on Earth. It is one of the microscopic green algae found in reservoirs of stagnant water. In the laboratory chlorella can be put in special open tanks, but obviously not on a spacecraft.

However, a compact and highly productive automatic incubator for chlorella has been created. Though many of the secrets of this vitally needed cell are still closed to us, scientists have proceeded as Ivan P. Pavlov did in his day when he began his study of the higher nervous systems of animals. He did not wait for each nerve cell to reveal its secrets, but tried instead to grasp the general rules of the workings of the brain.

Siberian scientists have experimented with the general rules of the behavior of chlorella. They learned, specifically, that it reacts to various stimuli—to light, or to a change in temperature. Out of dozens of factors affecting the algae's activities, they were able to isolate several main factors and to establish a system of control and regulation which could automatically maintain the regime necessary for the successful cultivation of chlorella.

After visiting a Siberian laboratory, a correspondent for *Izvestia* wrote that the chlorella incubator in no way resembled a hothouse. In appearance it was more like a chemical reactor, an enormous covered "lantern." The inside walls of the lantern are mirrored, almost blocking out the light of a powerful xenon lamp in the incubator. The chlorella live in a narrow 0.2-inch space between large layers of organic glass. The laboratory name for the lanterns is cuvettes, and like an old-fashioned collar they encircle the neck of the xenon lamp. With the xenon rays inside that green necklace the hidden process of photosynthesis takes place. In one test it was found that a cuvette with an overall surface of 90 square feet containing 1.1 pounds of chlorella could fully satisfy a man's oxygen needs.

For 30 days the algae incubator provided a tester with oxygen in exchange for her carbon dioxide. During that time, the algae reacted strongly to the behavior of their "partner"; while she slept, for example, the algae's life rhythms also slowed down.

Pass away, without water

Water makes up 60% to 65% of the weight of the human body. Losing even 10% of it is dangerous. Man can live without food quite a long time; without water he perishes in a few days.

The human organism must get 2 to 2½ quarts of water daily. This quantity can vary, depending on temperature changes in the environment, the work being done, the amount of food ingested, etc. Though he is working under extraordinary conditions, the cosmonaut must drink ordinary water, and the water problem is one of the most important in equipping for a space flight.

Before the first space launch doctors had to answer many questions: Can a cosmonaut drink water when he is weightless, what should it be stored in, how and in what quantity should it be taken, what should be its source? The first experiments on jet planes showed that in a condition of weightlessness water slips out of open containers, forms into small round balls, and begins to float around the cabin.

On Vostok the water supply was kept in a polyethylene-lined container fitted with a tube with a special mouthpiece. To get a drink one had to take the mouthpiece, press the button of a special locking mechanism, and then suck the water out.

None of the flights we know of have lasted more than 14 days, and for flights of such duration the water supply was sufficient. But can the water problem be solved on long space flights? For an interplanetary trip of several months or years, water will be necessary not only for drinking and food preparation, but also for sanitary-hygienic reasons, and of course 2 to 2½ quarts will not be enough.

Suppose each member of the team uses 4 quarts a

day (1.2 for drinking, 1 for preparing food, and 1.8 for sanitary needs). Then a team of six men on a one-month flight needs 720 quarts. To take so much weight on a flight is unadvisable. What then? Obviously the water manufactured by the organism—the sweat of the skin, the air it exhales—must be retrieved. A purification device will weigh several times less than the necessary quantity of liquid.

As the greatest quantity of liquid manufactured by the human organism is urine (1.2 to 1.4 quarts a day) scientists first set about trying to find a way to extract water from that product, and there is now a whole series of chemical and physical methods that can do this. For example, the sun's energy can be used to evaporate the urine at a high temperature, close to boiling, under low pressure (vacuum distillation).

If heat is not used to distill the urine, it can also be purified by heat's opposite. At low temperatures urine will form crystals of moisture which will produce pure water when melted. The low temperature of interplanetary space on the outer unsunlit surface of the rocket is adequate for such a purpose.

There was a report in the foreign press of an American scientist who tested the device under laboratory conditions and in eight hours extracted 4.5 quarts of water from urine. The liquid was evaporated in a separation column under low pressure, and the steam was drawn into a special compartment where the various toxic substances decomposed. The purified steam was then condensed and the water produced met all sanitary and hygienic requirements. Clinical analysis found no organic disturbances in those who drank the water over a long period of time.

Similar research has been done in our country. In 1958 a Soviet scientist, V. I. Danileiko, extracted potable water from urine with an evaporator. Interestingly enough, everyone who drank this "Vichy" enjoyed it—so long as they didn't know how it had been prepared! Only after they were told of its preparation did they begin to feel unwell. But that is already in the field of psychology, not physiology.

Ionic filters have also been used to purify urine. But these filters remove all salts, and since in urine purification it is not really distilled water that is wanted, but drinking water with a certain component of vital mineral salts, this is not the best method.

We know that the basic component of urine is urea. It represents from 80% to 90% of all urine's solid substance. This dangerous chemical substance can be treated by biological methods (microorganisms) or by biologically active substances (soybean ferments) and urea will separate into ammonia, carbonic acid and water. So in the closed ecological system on the spacecraft we have yet another recirculation of water.

In preparing for long-distance space flights the fact must be taken into account that man manufactures 10% more water daily than he requires. In addition, there is the oxidation of food products. So if cosmonauts are going to eat only products taken from Earth and not the produce of a closed ecological system, then the water supply is going to increase in direct proportion to the decrease in food supply.

For normal life conditions in the cabin of a spacecraft some sort of setup for hand and face washing and showers is also needed. Since water in weightlessness flies around in balls, shower stalls could be installed on the spacecraft where water could be pressurized.

But most of all engineers must think of economy. The whole system must be small in weight and size, must require a minimal amount of energy and work automatically. A small self-sustaining system that will work under conditions of weightlessness is not an easy assignment.

Meals in orbit

The crackers we were living on turned to dust mixed with worms, dirtied by rats and giving off an unbearable odor. . . . We ate the hide that covers the mast to protect it from the ropes. The hide was so tough we had to soak it in sea water for four or five days, then we cooked it over the coals and ate it. We often ate sawdust; and rats, repulsive as they are, became such a delicacy that we paid half a gold ducat apiece for them.

That was a quotation from the diary of one of the members of the first round-the-world voyage, Antonio Pigaletti.

Hunger! It has kept many a fanatically heroic explorer from his goal. But in the endless reaches of the ocean, the sandy wastes, exhausted by hunger and thirst, men have not lost hope. Dark clouds have brought long-awaited rain, animals and plants have appeared to provide him with food. Finally, help could always come from other people.

Now the great geographical discoveries are behind us. Modern expeditions are excellently equipped with all the vital necessities and men are no longer threatened by the fate of the first explorers. The conquering of space can be compared to the epoch of the great geographical discoveries. But the situation in which the new Columbus finds himself is vaster and more frightening than that of the explorers on Earth. The black depths of space are lifeless. Getting any kind of food if the supplies run out is impossible.

Before the start of the space flights scientists were interested in knowing not only what the cosmonaut could eat but if he could take food at all. They were especially concerned that crumbs of food scattering around the cabin under the condition of weightlessness might get into the respiratory systems of the cosmonauts and interfere with respiration. To answer this question they closely studied men eating under conditions of temporary weightlessness on airplanes. Pilots tried eating small pieces of meat, bread, and other solid foods. It turned out that pieces of dry food did fly out into the cabin and begin to soar about.

The food for the first two Vostok flights was prepared in the form of pâté, sauce, and purée packed in 6-ounce tubes. There were also tubes of processed cheese, chocolate sauce, coffee with milk. Aside from the puréed items, there were solid foods: sausage, lemon drops, and bread baked in small balls that would not have to be chewed.

The captain of the first, one-orbit Vostok flight did not have time to get hungry, but according to plan he took food anyway. Titov was in orbit a whole day and reaching into the food containers he got out the first tube. On Earth it weighed approximately 6 ounces, in space it weighed nothing. The tube contained puréed soup which he squeezed into his mouth like toothpaste. In the same manner he ate a second tube of meat and liver pâté and drank some black-currant juice. Several drops came out and hung like berries in front of his face. He found it interesting watching them, barely moving, floating in the air. He picked them up with the tube stopper and swallowed them.

The experience of the first two space flights permitted an expansion of the food assortment. Various kinds of meats were included in the cosmonauts' rations: fried meats, cutlets, tongue, veal, boneless chicken. There were also caviar sandwiches, sprat turnovers, fruits. For some, there was even dried fish.

Nourishment is not simply a matter of taking food. It is a complex psychological and physiological process. Even on a short flight, tasty and favorite foods can ease the tension of a cosmonaut's work. Equally important are the circumstances under which food is taken—a clean tablecloth, pretty dishes, soft music, easy conversation, all make a man relax over his food. On the other hand, tasteless, unappetizing food and bad service can be irritating, prevent relaxation, and halt the flow of digestive juices.

On the Vostok and Voskhod flights there were of course no dining rooms, no wide choice of delicious foods, but there was pleasant company. Egorov told of one space meal: "We spent the flight unstrapped and unharnessed, sitting and resting back in our chairs, changing positions, changing places even, moving about as we wished. During our meal we took our weightless food not just with our hands but tried catching it with our mouths. It was sort of a hunt we made not just for fun, but also to analyze weightlessness. It was very funny though, and we were laughing throughout the whole meal. When the medical equipment came down and floated in front of us, we called it our 'sputnik.' We had our light moments on that flight."

When fresh food was included in the cosmonauts' rations, the question arose of how to keep it for several days without refrigeration. The food was vacuum-packed in cellophane and well sealed, a perfectly acceptable method, but only for short flights.

On flights of less than six months Soviet scientists consider a full supply of food from Earth advisable, provided the weight and volume of foodstuffs can be kept minimal. For this there is the process called lyophilization—dehydration and compression. It must be admitted that such food does not arouse ecstasy, but that is just another sacrifice demanded by science.

The Moon and the orbital space stations of the distant future may be able to get food from Earth by rocket taxis. But what is the answer for interplanetary flights?

As we know, when a man is in a state of calm—lying in bed let us say—to maintain normal vital functions he requires energy equal to 1500–1700 calories per day. When he is at work his expense of energy rises significantly. For example, heavy physical labor uses up 5000–6000 calories per day. Light work (and from the point of view of energy the work of the cosmonauts in flight can be considered light) uses up around 3000 calories a day.

How much food is needed to replace such energy expenditures? These are the figures: 1 carbohydrate gram or 1 protein gram burned by the organism represents 4.1 calories. (One ounce = 28.35 grams.) Fats are more valuable: 1 gram of fat oxidized in the organism represents 9.3 calories. The simplest thing would seem to be to take 11 ounces of pure fat, pack it as compactly as possible, and a man's daily requirement would be taken care of.

But food is not just a source of energy, it is the building material necessary for the constant renewal of the organism and this requires proteins. Science has established the best ratio for food intake. A good ratio is four parts carbohydrates, one part protein, one part fat. A man doing light physical work should get 14 ounces of carbohydrates, 3.5 ounces of protein, 3.5 ounces of fat daily—21 ounces in all, not including water. Imagine then how much food an expedition to Mars, for example, would require. The trip there and back would take several years and every pound of concentrated food taken from Earth would cost more than a pound of pure gold.

Clearly we must seek another way out. We know that matter does not disappear. The organism makes use not of food itself but its energy, and once the energy has been released, the complex organic compounds—proteins, fats, and carbohydrates—leave the organism in the form of simple elements—nitrogen, carbon, hydrogen, calcium, phosphorus. The logical thing would be to synthesize these simple elements back into compounds which could again be used by man. If this were to be done on a space flight, only a few pounds of those elements would be required for each member of the team. Unfortunately at the present level of science and technology such a synthesis is not practicable, although possible in principle.

Once again Tsiolkovskii's hothouse comes to our aid. As we have said, experiments on earth have already closed the ring of a closed ecological system for the exchange of gases and the rotation of water. Only the last link in the cycle now remains: the use of the organism's wastes for the production of food.

Tsiolkovskii's idea for the rotation of elements by means of photosynthesis on board rockets was first realized by his successor, the Soviet scientist F. A. Tsander. "In 1926," he wrote, "I cultivated some plants in a glass of water, fertilized in a ratio of 1:200." Taking the factor of weightlessness into consideration, Tsander suggested that it would be possible to cultivate plants on a space flight without the water, simply by sprinkling the roots with a nutrient solution, that is to say to achieve aeration.

By this method, Tsander wrote, "All wastes could be put back into use within 24 hours. From a hothouse such as this, filled with pure oxygen and carbon dioxide and kept at high temperature obtainable from interplanetary space, one could expect very good harvests."

Having conducted numerous experiments, scientists have come to the conclusion that unicellular algae would be most suitable for use in space. The higher plants use only 1% of the energy received from the sun while some algae use up to 10%. In addition they are fully capable of "reworking" the organic wastes of men and animals, restoring them to fats, proteins, and carbohydrates by the process of photosynthesis, thus completing ecological rotation.

Chlorella has convincingly demonstrated its advantages over and over. It not only purifies the atmosphere but is itself a source of food. One quart of chlorella suspension provides nutritive matter consisting of 50% protein, 25% fat, 15% carbohydrates, 10% mineral salts, with vitamins A, B, and C. Just 250 quarts of algae culture will supply man with oxygen, water, and food for a long time.

But can the organism tolerate such food? In 1954 the American scientists Tink and Harold fed algae to rats for a period of 120 days. This had no negative effect on the test animals; they developed exactly like their fellows in the control group. In the United States and in our country we have experimented with algae in man's diet. The algae did not go unnoticed; there were complaints that the food was tasteless and smelled bad, and there were stomach upsets. It became obvious that food on interplanetary flights could not be limited to algae alone.

The experiments are still going on. Biologists are trying to include higher plants in a closed ecological system along with the algae. In the hothouses of future spaceships we'll be able to raise all kinds of vegetables such as cucumbers, peas, tomatoes, and potatoes.

Of his experiments in cultivating such plants under conditions similar to space conditions Tsander wrote: "I cultivated peas, cabbage, and several other vegetables in charcoal, which is three to four times lighter than ordinary soil. My experiments proved that charcoal can be used when fertilized with the appropriate fertilizer."

It is probable that animals too will find their use. Of special interest among the lower animals is plankton, as well as the smaller crustaceans—daphnia and cyclops—though it is not yet known how they would affect the organism if they were taken as food over a long period. Among the higher animals chickens and rabbits would be best suited for long flights: they grow and reproduce rapidly and need relatively little food. Their food could be algae, plant greens, their own crushed eggshells, and ground bones.

Scientists are still working on the idea of the rotation of elements on board a rocket envisioned by Tsiolkovskii. Much has still to be done with problems in the preparation of food under conditions of weightlessness, and the problem of the inevitable odors. But much more complicated will be arriving at the necessary biological equilibrium among the people, animals, and plants; arriving, that is, at a mutually beneficial rhythm of life processes. There will have to be a biochemical balance of respiration rate between man and plant, and a strict correlation between food production and food consumption by the cosmonauts.

Sensory starvation

On March 24, 1896, the first radiogram in history, consisting of two words—"Heinrich Hertz"—traveled a distance of 800 feet.

In 1900 the wireless telegraph invented by A. S. Popov first found practical usage by the Russian fleet when the battleship *General-Admiral Apraksin* was rescued from the rocks.

Radio has continued to serve man ever since. Of course other means of communication have been continued and perfected so that on Earth one can transmit information by wire and by cable laid across the ocean floor. But on space flights there is no alternative: radio is the only thing connecting the cosmonaut to his planet.

On Vostok there were two shortwave telegraphic-telephonic transmitters, working on frequencies of 15.765 and 20.0006 megahertz, capable of relaying information a certain distance. But when the ship was flying over the territory of the U.S.S.R. radio contact had to be made with the help of a third ultrahigh-frequency transmitter. Shortwave transmitters provide good radio contact over short distances as the diffusion of their radio waves is almost unaffected by the ionic strata of the atmosphere and is less sensitive to interference, but they are of little use in the vast distances of space.

Transmission from Earth to the spaceship was also made by one UHF and two shortwave transmitters. Radio operators all over the U.S.S.R. tuned in to Vostok, depending on where it was at any given moment. Also on board Vostok was a tape recorder which the cosmonaut turned on every time he started to speak. As he flew over the U.S.S.R. the tape could be transmitted to Earth.

Thus Yuri Gagarin was able to maintain constant two-way contact with Earth for the entire flight until the spaceship reentered the dense strata of the atmosphere. According to him, audibility was excellent.

The voices of his comrades in the tracking stations sounded as distinct as if they were right beside him. When the spaceship was in orbit, Earth wanted to know what he could identify down below. The answer was, the same things that are clearly visible from a jet plane flying at high altitude—mountain ridges, great rivers, massive forests, islands, ocean shorelines.

During the group flights, Andrian Nikolaev, Pavel Popovich, Valerii Bykovskii, and Valentina Tereshkova talked not only with Earth but among themselves. To the credit of our radio engineers, audibility was very good at all times.

In addition to radio contact there was television. By signal transmitter the cabin received telemetric information about the workings of various systems in the propulsion module and instructions from Earth concerning the guidance of spaceship systems.

When man sets out for other planets radio contact will be infrequent—but all the more important. It will be the only thread connecting the cosmonauts to Earth. Just how precious that thread is can be seen in the diary Valentina Tereshkova kept while undergoing a test of nervous-psychic stability in an isolation chamber. (The discussion of the experiments in the isolation chamber and the analysis of the results were written with O. N. Kuznetsov.) In this experiment Tereshkova was completely cut off from the outside world, with no information coming into the chamber. She was required to report her sensations and feelings periodically by radio. The contact was one-way, unreciprocated.

Here is what we read in the diary: "I thought about how precious the radio must be to the space pilot, that frail thread connecting him to Earth. How tensely he must listen to the dying sounds, how melancholy to think of them down there with their feet on the ground, all together, with nothing threatening them! And I ... if I feel this way sitting on Earth, up there it must be a million times stronger."

Under ordinary circumstances man has no reason

to complain of a lack of sense impressions. Every day his eyes open to hundreds and thousands of different pictures. All sorts of sounds play ceaselessly on his ears, creating a continuous acoustical background. The skin experiences changes in temperature and movement of the air. The sensory organs receive all manner of impressions and nerve impulses send on the information to the brain. While it is true that far from all the irritants are consciously understood by man, they are necessary for the normal working of the brain.

If the constant irritants are lacking there can be serious functional loss. For example, a Russian therapist of the last century, S. P. Botkin, described a patient who had lost sensory feeling everywhere but on the skin of one hand. This patient slept all the time and was aroused only by a touch on her "feeling" hand.

Pavlov observed a patient who as the result of an injury had, of all his sense organs, only one eye and one ear in operation. He had only to close these windows on his inner world, and he immediately sank into deep sleep.

Pavlov conducted a number of experiments on dogs in "a tower of silence" and came to the conclusion that a constant flow of nervous impulses coming from the sensory organs to the cortex is necessary for the normal operation of the brain. A monotony of impressions due to an insufficient flow of outside irritants sharply lowers the energy level, or tone, of the cortex, and this can lead to disturbances of psychic functions. The term in space psychology for this shortage of irritants to the brain from the environment is "sensory starvation." Research in isolation chambers has shown that this starvation puts man's psyche to a difficult test.

On long interplanetary flights the cosmonauts will inevitably run up against a similar phenomenon. For months they will see around them only the bright unblinking stars against the black bottomless sky and the blinding disk of the unsetting Sun. There will be no day, no night, no winter, no summer. From the moment the rockets are fired, the cosmonauts will be in a sphere of silence. There will be only the feeble sounds of the electrical apparatus to break the silence in the cabin.

Of course while they are working the cosmonauts will have sensory impressions enough: they must guide the spaceship, make scientific observations and reports. But for the leisure hours there will be a sensory deficit—one, however, that modern technology can eliminate. There will be specially selected color films and books on board. It may be possible to put a whole library on film that can be projected on a screen large enough so the text can be read without strain. In the rest compartment they'll probably be able to create an effect of nature with a stereoscope and recordings of birdsongs and the whirring of grass-hoppers.

A special role in the battle against sensory starvation will fall to the two-way UHF radio and television transmitters. With their help cosmonauts will always be able to follow life on Earth, "go to the theater," movies, sports events, see and talk with their family and friends.

Experience has shown that music is a great weapon against sensory starvation. Its highly emotional effect can improve man's mood and increase his working efficiency. Spaceships will be able to get music either on a phonograph or on radio.

We have made studies of the effect of music on the condition of sensory starvation. Specifically, we have unexpectedly played excerpts from musical works in an isolation chamber, simultaneously registering the subject's physiological response by which we could judge his emotional state as well. The arias of Susanin, Prince Igor, and Konchak from the famous Glinka and Borodin operas were played for one subject who listened to the arias calmly, with his eyes closed. Later he reported that the arias had called forth sharp memory images of one or the other opera and he said that he could actually see the scene and opera singers.

Another subject, when told about the experiment, asked to hear Mephistopheles' songs, Figaro's and Prince Igor's arias, and a popular song. When they were played for him, it was Prince Igor's aria that made the strongest impression. As he listened, his posture and facial expression changed: he became deeply concentrated, his face expressed great emotion, tears ran down his cheeks.

An even sharper reaction was observed with a woman subject. The experiment in the isolation chamber unexpectedly finished with Rachmaninoff's *First Concerto for Piano and Orchestra.* Though Rachmaninoff was known to be one of her favorite composers the effect was still startling. Practically from the first moment the girl went numb, her eyes stopped moving and then filled with tears, her breathing became deep and uneven. Her emotion was so strong that a laboratory worker observing the experiment became frightened and cried to the doctor in charge: "What are you doing? Stop the experiment! She's ill!"

At the conclusion of the experiment the subject gave her report: "It was a perfectly extraordinary state. I felt as if I were being strangled by tears and that in another moment I would break down and cry. In order not to cry I started breathing deeply. It was as if all my family, friends, previous life, and dreams were rushing past me. Actually, it wasn't the images themselves that upset me but a whole complicated set of feelings having to do with my relationship to life. Then the painful feelings began to subside, the music became pleasant, and its beauty and completeness made me calm again."

The experiments with music on a condition of sensory starvation uncovered one general rule—the heightening of the emotional-esthetic response, and it will be important on space flights that the members of the team have the chance to listen to music. The question of dosage, however, also needs research, for we know that an excess of music can evoke negative reactions. Instead of bringing joy and pleasure, the noblest art sometimes brings only suffering.

The musicologist S. Mezhinskii has written: "There is no end of listeners who listen to the radio from morning to late at night but it is only superficial listening. In reality, for such a person the sounds of the radio are just floating aimlessly in the air and the content of the music does not reach him. A surfeit of music and singing is harmful to man's esthetic training, prevents a genuine penetration into the world of art, and gradually gives birth to emotional indifference and esthetic deafness."

Space armor

> For a period of six months I lowered 100 men to a depth of 100 to 130 feet and I watched 200 foreign divers doing the same thing under the same conditions. All the divers were breathing air pressurized to 4 or 5 atmospheres. Five men died and an enormous number sustained various afflictions, the worst of which were paralysis of the legs, bladder trouble, deafness, and anemia. Men raised too quickly got sick. . . . No one died in the water, only after coming out of the water. They would begin to complain, mostly about their hearts, lie down on the deck of the barge, and after several hours they would die.

This was written in 1872 by Deneiuruz, the designer of a ventilated diving suit. The reader may wonder what relevance underwater diving has to a space flight. There is a connection.

It became clear afterward that the cause of the divers' deaths had been the bends, or as it is now called, caisson disease. The organism of a diver deep under water is affected by increased air pressure. Air solution takes place in his blood and tissues, specifically of the basic tissue component nitrogen. The longer a man is under pressure and the deeper he goes (for every 10 yards the pressure increases by 1 atmosphere) the higher the concentration of dissolving gases in his blood.

If he then rises quickly to the surface, that is to say, if decompression take place too quickly, the gas in his blood and tissues begins to rush out of the organism like gas from an opened bottle of champagne. Bubbles form in the blood vessels of the vitally important organs and the man either dies or is paralyzed.

Properly speaking, all the Earth's inhabitants are "submarines" in an ocean of air. We have on us a constant air pressure of 14.7 pounds per square inch, with a fairly large amount of air dissolved in the organism. But if we were too quickly raised to the surface of that ocean of air, the same thing would happen to us as to the divers drawn too quickly out of the ocean depths. Aeroembolism would result.

The idea of testing animals at high "altitudes" began in 1640 with the inventor of the mercury thermometer, the Italian physicist Torricelli. He put animals in test tubes, created a vacuum inside with the mercury, and established that animals will die in a rarefied atmosphere.

In 1650 the Magdeburgian physicist Herich invented the vacuum pump, which made it possible for Robert Boyle to study the effect of lowered barometric pressure on various physical bodies and living organisms. In 1670, Boyle wrote:

> Little bubbles generated upon the absence of the air in the blood, juices, and soft parts of the body may by their vast number and their conspiring distension variously strengthen in some places and stretch in others the vessels, especially the smaller ones that convey the blood and nourishment; and so by choking up some passages and vitiating the figure of others, disturb or hinder the due circulation of the blood. . . . And to show how this production of bubbles reaches even to very minute parts of the body, I shall add on this occasion . . . what

may seem somewhat strange, what I once observed in a viper furiously tortured in our exhausted receiver, namely that it had manifestly a conspicuous bubble moving to and fro in the waterish humor of one of its eyes.

Boyle's experiments showed that extremely low barometric pressure is fatal to the living organism.

Man in space lives in a pressurized cabin in conditions close to those on Earth, but the possibility of the cabin's becoming depressurized cannot be excluded, should, for example, the spaceship collide with a micrometeorite. There have been some minor collisions with very small micrometeorites which caused no especial damage to the spaceship. But when a meteorite weighs $\frac{1}{10}$ ounce it becomes a real danger. A meteorite weighing even $\frac{1}{30}$ ounce and flying at a speed of 100 to 130 feet per second could hit a mass five times its size with a force equal to an explosion.

When we were preparing to put our first man in space much attention was devoted to the danger of meteorites. The Vostok space suit was designed by our engineers with them in mind. In the first place the space suit had to protect the life and working efficiency of the cosmonaut in the event of cabin depressurization. Then it had to isolate man from the atmosphere of the cabin if for some reason toxic elements materialized in the air; keep him afloat in water; protect him from the cold if he landed in a cold region; and be adaptable for the catapult and descent. Finally, the space suit had to protect the cosmonaut from injury if he landed in a forested or mountainous area.

The first man in space had a polyester space suit of the ventilated type consisting of three layers, each of which was a complete suit. The outer or protective layer had the equipment for adjusting the pressure in the suit. Then came the pressurized suit and under that an insulated suit with the ventilation system. Over everything went a colorful orange cover and a life preserver to keep him afloat in the case of a splashdown in the sea or ocean.

The helmet of the space suit had a visor made of double glass which the cosmonaut could open and close. In appearance the helmet was very like the headpiece of a knight of the Middle Ages, with its movable visor. The gloves of the space suit could be removed, but when they were on, the whole system was completely pressurized.

On ,a normal flight the cosmonaut works without his gloves. But let us suppose that the cabin is hit by a meteorite. The air inside the cabin instantly streams out through the aperture into space and the pressure in the cabin drops catastrophically. These are the most dangerous seconds.

In the foreign press several episodes of airplane depressurization at high altitudes have been described. There the fall in barometric pressure did not cause serious damage to the plane as there was not an absolute vacuum outside. Yet the rush of air was so powerful that it took with it not just small objects but even passengers. One passenger on a plane flying over the Atlantic was drawn right through the window.

When depressurization by explosion was reproduced in an altitude chamber the cosmonauts first experiencing it lost control and went into a kind of trance. They stopped working and did not react to orders. But soon they returned to normal, and realizing the situation they began to respond rationally.

Several seconds does not seem a long time. But in the event of cabin depressurization time is measured not in seconds but in fractions of seconds. Can anything be done in that amount of time? Is it possible for a man to prepare himself? Aviation experience has convinced us that it is possible. The pilot preparing for a flight must experience depressurization himself in specially equipped altitude chambers and live through everything involved.

But what if the cosmonaut is sleeping or distracted by some activity? In that case the space suit is equipped with an automatic device located in the helmet. It starts the emergency ventilation which circulates the air from the cylinders in the body of the space suit and a mixture of oxygen and air or pure oxygen in the helmet. A special regulator maintains the pressure in the space suit at the necessary level.

It is not just in altitude chambers that the space-suited cosmonauts get the training. They make parachute jumps, coming down on land and water. If on water, the suit is buoyant and a man in a space suit can survive more than 12 hours without feeling the cold. The Voskhod team did not train in their suits, but in light sports costumes.

The space suit is necessary on a space flight. Members of the team frequently have to leave the ship to walk in space and check or repair the ship or an orbital station. And you can't set foot on the moon or any other planet without a suit.

A special space suit was required for the first walk in space. It was constructed differently from the others; it weighed less and was easier to move about and work in. And although it was lashed to the spaceship, its oxygen supply was autonomous.

How did Aleksei Leonov, our first man to walk in space, feel?

We knew [he said], that the first experimental walk in space would be complicated and would have to be very carefully executed. We went strictly according to schedule on that exit operation and made precise observations of the sequence of events. The walk in space was made with a backpack containing an autonomous life-supply unit. The backpack was strapped on in the cabin just before going to the hatch. All the life-supply systems of the ship and the backpack, the medical recording instruments and the space suit were checked out again and again. The pressure in the space suit could be kept at 0.4 or 0.27 atmosphere.

Out in space I felt just fine, I was in a good mood. Reentering the spaceship represented no particular difficulty unless you count the trouble with the camera. But that had nothing to do with the space suit.

More complicated will be the "space armor" cosmonauts will wear in order to land on the Moon, Mars, and other celestial bodies. British specialists see the Moon space suit in the form of a suit shelter made of two aluminum cylinders with an air-conditioning and -purification system, a seat for resting on, mechanical hands, radio apparatus, sources of energy, supplies of food, water, etc.

In other versions of the Moon suit the supplies of water and oxygen, the sources of electrical energy, and the radio apparatus will be stored in a special locomotive cart which the cosmonaut can also use to ride in.

Then there are the American experiments with suits for the surface of the Moon in the Apollo project. One of them weighs 21 pounds and is calculated for a pressure of 0.35 atmosphere, an emergency pressure of 0.246 atmosphere, and has a supply of pure oxygen. Its completely autonomous life-supply systems will be strapped to the astronaut's back before he leaves the spaceship and can work uninterruptedly for four hours. On Earth the apparatus weighs 31 pounds.

It must be remembered that while these suits seem bulky and heavy, they will feel different on the Moon where they will weigh one-sixth of what they do on Earth.

Robinson Crusoes in space

History is rife with incidents of shipwreck and people who have wound up as Robinson Crusoes on Earth's uninhabited islands. But what would happen in space if there were to be a spaceship wreck, where an island would be only a dream?

The flight of the spacecraft Voskhod-2 went strictly according to plan until it was time to land. The automatic control failed, the spacecraft made another orbit, and Pavel Belyaev and Aleksei Leonov had to land it by manual controls far from the designated area. They were surrounded by forest in deep snow and the cold was intense. The cosmonauts hooked up their ground radio and informed the search team of their whereabouts. Planes and helicopters arrived and the "victims" were evacuated to Baikonur where the trip had begun.

But if the evacuation had been delayed for some unforeseen reason they could have held out quite a long time, for they had their Emergency Reserve Supply—the ERS survival kit known to all travelers. We no longer know which of the sea or land explorers first had the idea for a supply of food and equipment to be used only in an extreme eventuality which could happen to anyone who must work or live far from populated areas, in the sea, forest, or mountains.

The specific contents of the ERS depend on the geographical conditions of the expedition. Cold, one of the worst factors, is a cause of much suffering. Exposure, frostbite, prolonged time in cold water or penetrating winds all can mean death. Therefore, pilots flying to the pole are given warm clothing, sleeping bags, fuel, inflatable rubber boats and rafts with waterproof covers. In addition to the climate, there is the threat of attack by polar bears, so men are given guns and ammunition for protection from attack and hunting food.

Given a limited supply of potable water, heat is no less a danger. Dehydration and overheating of the body can have disastrous consequences. A loss of 10% to 15% of the body's water means a drop of efficiency and a loss of more than 20% is fatal for many people. The first question to be solved in the design of lifeboats is that of a fresh-water supply.

When the automatic control on Voskhod-2 failed, the captain was able to choose his landing area and come down out of orbit over a specific square of Earth's surface. But had the cabin become depressurized the cosmonauts would have had no time for lengthy deliberation and would have had to land the ship in nothing flat. Who knows where they might have landed—in the Sahara, in the jungle, in the northern wastes. They would probably have landed on water, which occupies so large a part of the Earth's surface. In an emergency, in other words, they could land practically anywhere.

Therefore the problem arises of designing an ERS that will protect a man's life until he is rescued in any geographical zone and at the same time be compact and light.

A cosmonaut's ERS doesn't look very large, but when its contents are taken out you feel as if you are watching a magician pull yards of material, ribbons, flowers, a water carafe, then maybe a goose or a dove out of one small cylinder. The inflatable rubber boat in a cosmonaut's ERS can be filled to the top with the rest of the contents.

Bailing out in an emergency, a man can never be completely insured against harm. He can be scratched, cut up, or, worse, become sick. Therefore, medical supplies, bandaging materials, and medicines are included in the ERS and the box in which they are packed "can be used as a frying pan" as it says on the top.

A portable stove can be used to make hot meals. There are briquettes of fuel if no other fuel can be found and water- and windproof matches.

Finding himself in a cold region, the cosmonaut must first of all see to his shelter. For this he can use not only tree branches but his parachute. As snow has good insulatory properties, it is possible to dig a cave in the snow and floor it with dry grass, branches, or the parachute. The inflatable boat can also serve as a bed. Landing in a hot region, the cosmonaut must immediately remove his space suit and change into the light clothing included in the ERS.

In any emergency situation a fire is necessary for warmth, for signaling, and for preparation of food.

There is nothing particularly complicated about a fire except that you must be able to build one in any weather. It was discovered during the training period that the best fire builders were hunters and fishermen, so hunting and fishing were included in the circle of the cosmonauts' activities. Aleksei Leonov was the head of the hunting team.

The cosmonaut has to know not just what country he has landed in but how to pinpoint his position accurately in whatever corner of the globe fate has thrown him, and for this he has a compass, sextant, and maps. He has equipment to set up two-way radio contact, with a battery capable of working under any climatic conditions.

A man cannot always be seen from the air even when visibility is good. But the task of finding him is simplified by the use of signal rockets and pocket lanterns and the bright orange of the space suit also helps to attract attention. In case of splashdown there is a packet of dyes which when spread on the water form a large, easily seen fluorescent spot.

Then there is the question of food and water. Given today's level of technology victims of a crash are usually found within a few hours so there is no need to strictly limit the consumption of food and fluids. On the contrary, it is important to eat normally after a crash to keep up the strength being spent on building a camp and setting up a signal system. A knowledgeable and experienced person should be able to get food for himself almost anywhere on the planet. One pilot lost in a crash in the tundra subsisted exclusively on pigeons and fish caught from the lake. When he was found, his survival kit was intact.

The whole world is familiar with the heroic trip made by the French doctor Alain Bombard, who crossed the Atlantic in a rubber raft without food or water. With this brilliant and difficult experiment he showed that the main reason people perish at sea is fear and confusion. A man can survive if he has the willpower, if he knows how to get food and how to use salt water. The cosmonauts' ERS has fishing tackle as well as a boat in case of a splashdown.

Food supplies can be supplemented by hunting, but this is hunting with a difference. In uninhabited regions where his life is at stake, a man must hunt, not for the usual ducks and rabbits, but for such creatures as gophers, turtles, frogs, lizards, even edible snakes. These he can hunt without firearms, simply using snares or his bare hands, but he has a pistol for deer, walrus, seal, etc., and to protect him from predatory creatures.

Two cosmonauts, "dropped" in a forest to be tested in an emergency situation, discovered that a pistol is harder to aim than a hunting rifle. It was January and the cold was fierce. The "victims" made camp, built their shelter out of poles, branches, and parachutes, covered it with snow, started a fire, and established radio contact. On the second day of Crusoedom a rabbit was put into their area. The cosmonauts decided to shoot it and have a meal of fresh meat. They both started shooting, but missed again and again. Having used up all their ammunition they had to resort to their canned goods in the ERS. After that our cosmonauts could be found on the practice range, learning to shoot pistols.

Man at the controls

What does the control panel on Vostok look like? There is an instrument panel showing humidity, temperature, and composition of the air in the cabin, and readings on all the different systems on the ship. The position of the plane and target area are indicated on a globe spinning at the speed of the Earth and it tells the cosmonaut where he is when the retro-rockets are fired.

The cosmonaut can ascertain his position in space by means of the periscope in front of him and by the windows to the right and behind him.

The control panel also has switches regulating the

window blinds, the radio transmitter, and the temperature. Here too are manual controls and retrorocket levers. On that board the pilot can check the workings of all the separate systems on the spaceship and on the basis of what he learns he can change any of the systems, even the orbit.

For a successful reentry the spaceship must move in a strictly designated attitude or it won't go out of orbit when the retro-rockets are fired, but will go into another orbit.

The spacecraft direction-control system on Vostok was automatic, and it set the spacecraft at a certain angle to the Sun. Optical and gyroscopic data were registered on an electrical computer connected to the thrusters. The retro-rockets were set to be fired at a certain time after the ship was in orbit. If the automatic control system had failed, the cosmonaut could have landed the spacecraft by means of the periscope and manual control of the side thrusters.

The periscope is made of two ring-shaped mirror reflectors, light filters, and a graticule. Light rays from the horizon hit the first reflector, pass through to the second glass, and through the graticule to the eye of the cosmonaut. When the spacecraft is yawing, to the cosmonaut the horizon is a circle, and he can see sections of the Earth's surface beneath him through the center of his window. The pitch of the spacecraft can be determined by the "flight" of the Earth's surface.

The cosmonaut thus has two kinds of activities on board ship: maintenance activities (monitoring the temperature and pressure in the cabin) and control activities (changing the direction of the spacecraft, landing it in an extreme emergency).

Before the space flights it was thought that manual controls would not be necessary. The automatic system gives the flight maximum chance of success and safety. But the most important systems are duplicated over and over again, and here man has a great role in controlling the ship. But this is a special theme which we'll turn to in the next chapter.

CHAPTER TWO

The Cosmonaut and the Robot

By the last third of the 20th century automatic controls have penetrated virtually all spheres of human activity. They can fly airplanes, run business operations, and complete various stages of industrial production. "Thinking" machines can write music, solve complex mathematical equations, translate foreign texts, diagnose illnesses.

But in spite of all that, in spite of cybernetics, the machine's work activities can only accomplish a specified goal, whereas man's work activities are qualitatively different. In transforming nature, man brings about consciously set goals, with the machine as an executor of his will, the tool of his labor. And of course the psychic and physiological processes that take place in a man at work are essentially different from the processes taking place in automatic operations. But the work of man and the work of a machine do have enough in common to permit a comparison between certain automatic functions in a machine and the eyes, ears, and the brain of a man.

Man or automaton?

When operating a machine—be it an automobile, airplane, or spaceship—a man is dealing with specific mechanisms. But he must first take in his environment and interpret the intelligence he receives from it. Nervous impulses run from the sensory organs to the brain which then assimilates the information and formulates the response. This process requires time, which experiments have shown varies from person to person, from 0.1 second to 0.2 second. More complicated responses—a certain button to be pressed in response to a light of a certain color—require 0.5 second or more.

The insufficient speed of human nervous psychic responses began to be felt in the space age. At speeds twice the speed of sound, the space around a plane is "blind" for the pilot, he cannot perceive it. Objects that appear to be 300 feet ahead of him are in actuality behind him. If two pilots are flying straight at each other at such speeds and one comes out of the clouds 700 feet ahead of the other he will not be able to see the other in time.

Experience has shown that the pilot of a jet plane requires approximately 1.5 to 2 seconds to estimate any ordinary situation. During that time a spacecraft traveling at 5 miles a second would have covered 7.5 to 10 miles. It would seem that at such speeds the cosmonaut would simply be unable to react to events taking place in space, to take in objects falling in his field of vision. This means that the controls of an interplanetary spacecraft can only be entrusted to an automaton.

But the first manned space flight showed that this was not quite so. Here is how the surrounding environment was perceived by Gagarin from the spacecraft window on that flight:

At an altitude of 200 miles the lighter surface of the Earth can be seen very well. Looking at Earth I saw clouds and cloud shadows lying on the fields, the forests, and the ocean. The water surfaces looked dark but with shiny spots. I could easily make out the continents, islands, big rivers, large reservoirs, land faults. I had never been higher than 50,000 feet before, and the visibility was worse than from a plane of course, but it was still very good. To tell the truth I was amazed that at that altitude the detail of the Earth's surface could be seen so well. The spacecraft was going close to 17,000 miles per hour, but the Earth's surface was right there in my field of vision outside the spacecraft window.

How can a man on a space flight see details of the Earth's surface or the even more distant stars? It seems the answer is space itself. If you look out the window of a fast-moving train at the embankment it is hard to make out anything but an unbroken blurry line, while more distant objects can be seen much more distinctly. There are three zones in the perception of separate objects: confluence, the glimpse or flash, and clear vision. It is knowing the borderline of confluence that helps the experienced pilot to estimate the distance to Earth when landing his plane.

The lower man flies over Earth, the more difficult it is for him to make out specific objects. The higher the orbit of the spacecraft the less aware he is of his speed (on an interplanetary flight the cosmonauts will lose the sense of speed altogether) and his vision becomes sharper and clearer.

When the spacecraft has moved away from Earth and into orbit a cosmonaut has a time "surplus" but in the event of collision with a heavenly body (a meteorite for example) or of an emergency landing, the cosmonaut will have *Zeitnot*—in the language of chess, his time will have run out.

Man's sensory organs are "grafted" onto a spacecraft in the form of radar and computers. They read signals from the environment, process the information, and give appropriate and simultaneous orders to the rockets—and they do this hundreds of times faster than man can do it.

There is another point. The maneuvers of a spacecraft moving along a collision course are not similar to the maneuvers of an aircraft in the atmosphere. Let us suppose that one airplane must overtake another. The pilot will increase his speed and bank the plane. To gain altitude he brings up the wing flaps, raising the lift of the wings to many times their lift in horizontal flight. But the rules of aerodynamics cease to operate in space. One spacecraft is trying to overtake another on the same orbit. If the pilot increases rocket power, he changes not just the speed of the flight but the parameters of the trajectory—and the craft goes into a higher orbit. Lower the speed, and it goes into a lower orbit.

Because man is incapable of making decisions with the split-second timing necessary in space maneuvers, he has the computer make them for him. But all the computer's indubitable skills have been prepared and given to it by man and it follows that it can give back only such information as it has been given. When it comes to unprogramed phenomena, it is in a blind alley. A computer cannot be programed for all eventualities, particularly for the analysis of the diversity of phenomena yet unknown to science that may be encountered in space.

Man has an advantage over the machine. He can take in information from his various sensory organs simultaneously and organize it into a whole. He has an enormous capacity for memory; that is to say, he can store information which, in the language of cybernetics, demands "minimal programing." Only man can abstract from his perceptions, make generalizations, and draw conclusions. He can reconstruct forms and events that have taken place in the past, and pass beyond the barrier of the present. He has the gift of foresight. In confronting an unknown phenomenon man can analyze it, drawing on his past experience, make a correct interpretation, and avoid unfortunate consequences.

At one time certain scientists maintained that man could not work in a state of weightlessness and solitude. They argued that the "loss" of weight would cause psychic reactions that would not only prevent him from working in space but even from living in space. The first space flight refuted these dismal prognoses:

"The transition into the state of weightlessness," the commander of a Vostok wrote, "I took very well. Although I had no assignment to take over the manual controls, there was much to be done in running the other systems of the spacecraft. I had the radio to operate, the window blinds to adjust, the controls to monitor, the flight log to fill out, and various other things to do. I became firmly convinced that a man in space could successfully handle the manual controls of his spacecraft."

Man is more flexible than a machine. The extent to which a machine can control a craft depends on its construction. The existing automatic regulators are strictly specialized. But through instruction and training man can "broaden his specialties" and learn how to run all kinds of systems, to change the programing by which the adjustments are made, and in the event of one or another system failing he can switch over to another system.

"But man is not a machine: he can get tired, bored, unhappy, and this inevitably has an effect on his control of the spacecraft," said a defender of the machine. "Machines are more reliable, they are indefatigable and steadier in their reactions to environmental forces." But this opinion too was refuted.

American specialists compared the reliability of various systems on board five spacecraft. One was operated by a man. He was supposed to take his instrument readings and manually control the attitude of the spacecraft. The other four systems were run by computers which had been duplicated two to five times for greater reliability.

At first all five systems worked equally well. But on the fourth day of the simulated space flights deviations became noticeable. After two weeks the doubly, triply, and quadruply duplicated systems could not be considered satisfactorily reliable. Nor could the quintuply duplicated system. The attitude of the craft operated by man showed very little deviation. If you calculate the enormous importance of weight on a spacecraft, the manned system wins hands down over its competition.

The role of man becomes particularly important in an emergency situation. When the American astronaut John Glenn's automatic control on Friendship-7 broke down, he had to land the craft by manual control. Afterward Glenn wrote: "My flight proved a number of things. Perhaps the most important lesson is that man belongs in space. Without him the spacecraft is deaf to the sounds and blind to the sudden problems and opportunities that present themselves.... Man has the reliability to operate the man-spacecraft combination and the adaptability to insert himself into the system and make it work. We never did consider the astronaut to be merely a passive passenger in Project Mercury. Now we know that man has a key role." The flight of Friendship-7 is a good proof of the principle. It could not have returned to Earth if there had not been a man on board.

The American astronauts are not the only ones who have run into trouble. When the automatic control broke down on Voskhod-2, Captain Belyaev took over, adjusted the direction of the spacecraft by manual control, and fired the retro-rockets at the designated time.

All this is convincing proof that no matter what the degree of automatization on a spacecraft, man will always play a governing and organizing role. Of course man cannot replace automatic controls, a space flight would be unthinkable without them. But at the contemporary level of science and technology it is better not to counterpose man versus the machine, but to search for more rational uses of human capacities and cybernetics. The machine must be controlled and directed by man, replacing him wherever it can be most effective. Then the control systems on spacecraft will become more reliable.

Foreign scientists have put the chance of an automatically controlled spacecraft getting to the Moon and back to Earth at 22%. For a manned flight, at 70%. If the pilot can correct troubles developing in the spacecraft systems, the chance rises to 93%.

Man with the assistance of automatic controls can more easily put a spacecraft into orbit, more accurately adjust the trajectory of the flight toward one or another planet and choose the proper place for a landing, than the automatic control can by itself. So the cosmonaut is an integral element in the operation of a highly automated technology. But the most rational use of man in the man-spacecraft combination is only attained when man's psychic-physiological propensities and the machine's technical characteristics are taken into consideration in constructing the spacecraft.

Man-machine

Engineering psychology studies the role of people operating various kinds of machines, viewing the operator as a link in the man-machine system. What is the man-machine system?

No matter what he is operating, an electric power station, a spacecraft, or a train, man's activities share a number of common traits. Before the appearance of the machine man could judge the results of his activities directly. Primitive man making himself a stone ax or a boat could see whether or not he was doing it right and correct himself as he went along if necessary. And today a bicyclist gets his information directly about the condition of the road, and he can feel the effect of his muscle power on the pedals and handlebars.

Remote control is a different matter. Now data are registered by transducers that relay information to instruments. It is with instrument readings that man has to deal. He decodes the information, makes a decision, and takes an appropriate action which can either be simple (pressing a button) or complex. But it is from man that the control signal comes, a signal that transforms the object, changing its state. This new state will be registered by the instruments which in turn will inform the operator. Thus man is in two-way contact with the object, assuming the role of regulator, a more responsible link in the closed circuit.

The development of automation will further separate man from the controlled unit and deprive him of direct control. Wedged in between his sensory organs and the controlled unit will be a whole set of technological mechanisms transmitting information, usually in code, which will be deciphered. The return response will be no more direct, but will go through many intermediate steps.

A curious situation develops. On the one hand man's job is made easier for him; many complex functions are transferred to the machine, broadening the range of problems that can be solved. On the other hand, the greater the part played by the machine and the more complex its functions become, the more imperative it is that its work be integrated. In other words, the relative role played by man becomes increasingly responsible.

As we have said, the operator learns from his instruments. But instrument reading has its own problems. Under ordinary circumstances, a pilot can see various objects on the Earth's surface which help him formulate his flight plan. He can depart from a given plan, and change his altitude without danger since he has his instruments before him and has visual points of reference (railroad tracks, a river, a television tower, etc.).

The situation changes when there are no such points of reference. Location in space cannot be taken from direct sensory impressions, but only from the instruments wedged in between the sensory organs and the environment.

The main difficulty is in deciphering the meaning of the signals in any concrete situation. Then, a pilot must not only be able to read the instruments correctly and draw inferences from the facts as applied to the actual situation but he must do it quickly, sometimes with lightning speed. He must also keep in mind where the aircraft has just been and where it will be in the near future.

On the orbital flights the cosmonauts were able to see the surface of the Earth through the windows of the spacecraft and determine what area they were over. Even when attitude control was totally automatic, the cosmonauts could still position their craft over the surface of the Earth by using a globe or map. Knowing their position by latitude and longitude, they could imagine the spot: desert, mountain, ocean, or forest. In other words they had a link with earthly points of reference. The train of thought could have run like this: Ten minutes ago I was over North Africa. Now I'm over the Black Sea. Ten minutes from now I'll be over the Urals.

Flights to other planets will require other more complicated trajectories, in a semielliptical curve joining two unfixed points moving in space at different speeds. Therefore navigation in space will take place according to a completely different set of coordinates. The system can be ecliptic, equatorial, horizontal, geocentric, heliocentric, or galactic. In any system Earth will remain the planet of departure and destination, but the spacecraft location will be derived from the stars, which will be the fixed points, whatever the coordinates.

Interplanetary spacecraft will move at cosmic speeds but in the immense vastness of the universe the speed will be insignificant. The starry heavens will seem frozen and still, no human sensory organ will be able to register the speed of the craft. The cosmonauts will figure the trajectory of their flight from the fixed points of the stars, feed the data into a computer which will then define the position of the spacecraft within the chosen system of coordinates. But man will no longer be able to position himself over the Earth's surface, he will have instead to imagine himself an "abstract point" in space, never before seen through any telescope.

When there's no feedback

Getting vital information from the environment is not always easy, as we have seen. Great difficulties lie in wait for the pilot who must switch from flying by instrument to flying by direct sensory observation. He begins to be hampered not so much by a lack of information as by a surplus. Pilots who have completed flights under difficult meteorological conditions have often suffered great damage to their nervous systems and been put into a highly neurotic state.

Having carried out a flying assignment at 20,000 feet, 33-year-old pilot L. was returning to the landing field and beginning a blind dive through the clouds. The plane had made it through the cloud curtain when it suddenly rocketed back up into the cloud, before coming down again and making a normal landing. "What happened?" the commanding officer asked the pilot. "Why did you blow it?" The pilot was pale and obviously upset. "It was like my mind exploded ... I don't remember anything ... like I lost consciousness although I know I didn't." Fortunately his condition had been of short duration and he had been able to land the plane, but the condition left traces. In the hospital he complained of sleeping badly, he was irritable and found all talk about what had happened to him very painful. When the doctors could discover no organic trouble, they came to the conclusion that it was a case of neurotic frustration. When the surplus information from the ground combined with the flood of information from his instruments the pilot had not been able to take the correct readings and quickly integrate them with the new sensory information. That demands a high level of training and self-control.

An analogous situation could arise on a space flight. For example, on the dark side of the Earth, the cosmonaut controls the direction of the spacecraft by instruments. Then coming out of the "night" he finds that he is able to observe objects on the Earth's surface directly, and like the pilot he must be able to integrate that information.

An operator must also know how correct he has been in his response to new information. Ignorance distresses man, makes him lose confidence in himself. An experiment was once conducted in an isolation chamber in which men were told to operate certain signals without any feedback to tell them if they were correct or not. The majority of them worked calmly; they were sure of themselves and unworried about the outcome of their decisions. But one man became disturbed and asked for the results. Receiving no answer, he repeated his request and then announced he was pressing the emergency button, the signal for terminating the experiment. The experiment was suspended and it was explained to the subject that had he made any blunders he would have known it immediately. As long as there was no signal it meant things were going along normally. The subject relaxed and the experiment caused no further emotional stress.

Similar psychological problems arise when there is no feedback from a machine and a man has no way of knowing what has happened. Gagarin ran up against this on the first space flight. According to plan, after the craft had orbited, the retro-rockets were to be fired and the capsule was to separate from the propulsion module and descend to Earth by parachute. While the spacecraft was on automatic control and the cosmonaut could monitor the instruments and receive information from the retro-rockets, he knew he could take over the manual controls in an extreme emergency. But once the separation of the propulsion module and the capsule had taken place, there was a communications blackout. The process took but a few dozen seconds, but his safe return to Earth depended on it. These were his feelings during those seconds:

After the retro-rockets were fired I waited for the separation of the propulsion module. This was over Africa. Just then the spacecraft rotated. Through the windows I saw Earth, then sky, from time to time the blinding rays of the Sun. The wait was terrible. It was as if time had stopped. Seconds felt like long minutes. But then the separation took place, and everything took its normal course.

Situations in which there is conflict with instruments are known in other professions as well. When operators at the controls of an electrical power station were studied it was found that even during "easy" watch, when there was nothing to be done but make sure that nothing broke down, electrical power station personnel experienced great nervous exhaustion. When the shift was over they were in no condition for mental activity; they were irritable and slept badly. The conclusion was obvious, not every man has the aptitudes of an operator. In the selection of the cosmonaut candidates, not only is physical health taken into consideration, but psychological aptitudes for work as an operator.

These aptitudes are determined by experiment. For example, there is a table with 49 squares numbered in no particular sequence in black (1 to 25) and red (1 to 24). The subject has to call out the numbers in order, black in ascending order and red in descending. Thus: 1-black, 24-red, 2-black, 23-red, etc. The task is far from easy and the person who can do it without making a mistake might well be compared to Napoleon who, they say, could do several things at one time.

The French psychologist Polan amazed his contemporaries when he demonstrated in 1897 that he could recite one poem and compose another at the same time, or figure out a complicated mathematical problem while reciting a verse. What enabled him to achieve such efficient productivity? The ability to switch his attention rapidly from one subject to another. This is precisely what an operator is required to do in a man-machine system, and this is why the experiment with the red-black table is so important.

Memory we know is a complex process. It is a reflection of reality, preservation of perception, reproduction or recognition of what was earlier perceived, experienced, or completed. Memory can be short-term (projective) or long-term. The importance of the latter needs no explanation: it represents the foundation of human erudition, of the systematic accumulation of knowledge. In Marshal Suvorov's words, "Memory is the storehouse of the mind, a storehouse with many shelves that must be filled with everything, wherever it will fit." Napoleon used to say that he had all knowledge stored in his head like a cabinet and that all he had to do was open the proper drawer to obtain needed information.

But no less important to the operator is short-term memory: it registers events as they take place, linking them in a chain with events having just taken place and forging the link with oncoming events. The operator must remember what state the operation was in before, what is happening to it now, and what can happen to it within a specified period of time.

When a man is searching, for example, for the black number 18, he cannot forget that he has just called out 8-red and that now he will have to find 7-red. Curiously enough, the greatest number of errors is made in the middle, when after 12-black and 13-red must follow 13-black and the 12-red. A continuity factor is at work in many operations with a specific program: in production, in transport, in sports. Within strict time limits, the strategic memory becomes increasingly important.

Let us consider the so-called "projection schemes." Before taking a certain action a man imagines that he is taking it and what the result will be. Having taken the action he collates the actual result with the projected one. Future action depends on the result of the collation; if there is a disparity then corrections can be made immediately.

Projection—a mechanism not yet fully understood—must be an internalized condition of any operative—and not only operative—activity, but it seems to be a mechanism very sensitive to obstacles, such as to prompting.

Here you have a teacher fluently reciting a verse to his class, a verse he knows very well. But if you try reciting the verse simultaneously with him but in another rhythm, he will quickly falter and begin to make mistakes.

Badly given commands from Earth can affect a pilot in the same way. He can become confused when several similar messages are transmitted simultaneously and he must choose what he needs to know from among a number of signals.

The black-red table was used in order to establish how steady the cosmonaut would be in confrontation with such obstacles. When the subject reached the most difficult middle section, a loudspeaker began reading off the same numbers in a slightly altered tempo. Those who were not obstacle-proof got lost and that put an end to the experiment.

K. S. Stanislavski once said about prompting: "In my opinion, a good prompter is one who can be quiet all evening and at the critical moment say the one word which has slipped from the actor's memory. But our prompter was hissing at you uninterruptedly and being a terrible bother. You didn't know what to do to get rid of that inordinately zealous helper who was trying to climb right through your ear and into your very soul. Finally he won, I lost my place. So I stopped and asked him not to bother me."

The difficulties involved in a man-machine system are far from exhausted.

The madness of instruments

Robot SPD 13 was near enough to be seen in detail now. His graceful, streamlined body threw out blazing highlights as he loped with easy speed across the broken ground. His name was derived from his serial initials, of course, but it was apt nevertheless, for the SPD models were among the fastest robots turned out by the United States Robot and Mechanical Men Corporation.

"Hey Speedy," howled Donovan and waved a frantic hand.

"Speedy!" shouted Powell. "Come here!"

The distance between the men and the errant robot was being cut down momentarily . . .

They were close enough now to notice that Speedy's gait included a peculiar rolling stagger, a noticeable side-to-side lurch, and then, as Powell waved his hand again and sent maximum juice into his compact head-set radio sender in preparation for another shout, Speedy looked up and saw them.

Speedy hopped to a halt and remained standing for a moment with just a tiny unsteady weave, as though he were swaying in a light wind.

Powell yelled, "All right, Speedy, Come here, boy."

Whereupon Speedy's robot voice sounded in Powell's earphones for the first time.

It said, "Hot dog, let's play games. You catch me and I catch you; no love can cut our knife in two. For I'm little Buttercup, sweet little Buttercup. Whoops!" Turning on his heel, he sped off in the direction from which he had come, with a speed and fury that kicked up gusts of baked dust.

And his last words as he receded into the distance were, "There grew a little flower 'neath a great oak tree," followed by a curious metallic clicking that might have been a robotic equivalent of a hiccup.

This passage was taken from a science-fiction story called "I, Robot," by an American writer and professor of biochemistry, Isaac Asimov. Asimov's robots frequently behave not just like thinking creatures but wise and sensitive ones. This is not pure fantasy. More and more often today in the professional literature you find electronic devices being characterized by such wholly human words as "fatigue," "training," and "behavior." These are not figures of speech, representing a kind of machine animism, they reflect the essence of a phenomenon. Any number of unforeseen chance happenings are possible in machine activities that sharply alter their "behavior." Sometimes it takes no more than a slight external pressure, a jolt, and within a short period of time an unexpected and seemingly causeless deviation will occur in the workings of an automatic mechanism. These deviations arising "of themselves," sometimes despite countermeasures, allow us to talk about the behavior of automatic mechanisms.

The following incident was a case in point. A bombing mechanism that refused to work in flight proved on the ground to be in perfect working order. But as soon as the plane attained a certain altitude, the instrument again "went on strike." The navigator became nervous and angry. It was particularly annoying that when the plane came down again to a certain level, the instrument began to work again and on coming to Earth the navigator was unable to prove the instrument's "guilt." The navigator's behavior seemed so peculiar that he was hospitalized and twice a psychiatrist was called in. The problem was solved only when the mechanism was "caught red-handed at the scene of the crime," with a photograph taken at the moment when it refused to work.

The possibility of unexpected reactions from instruments and automatic systems must especially be taken into consideration on space flights. Interplanetary spacecraft will be equipped with electronic self-regulating systems, systems which will adjust themselves optimally to changes in external and internal conditions. Such systems will not be intended for strictly planned programs. It follows that there will be more chance for surprise. The cosmonauts will have to know the possibilities for unreliable "behavior" in their electronic devices and be able to "diagnose" the instrument or mechanism that is "going out of its mind."

Ignorance of the technological particulars can be costly. When an operator stops trusting his instruments his nerves are put to a dangerous test.

Navigator Z., an experienced flier, was hospitalized for a neurotic condition: he'd become nervous, insomniac, and continually tired on flight assignments. He was particularly fatigued by practice bombing, which earlier he had enjoyed. It emerged that he had formerly worked on planes unequipped with automatic pilots, toward which his attitude was extremely negative. He considered them unreliable and was afraid that with "bad behavior" the plane would be taken to a place where bombing would not be possible. At first he simply didn't use the pilot, but when he was forced to submit to the discipline of using it, he began experiencing great nervous tension and fatigue, complaining of headaches and irritability. He continued using the pilot, turning it on much earlier than necessary. He was like the craftsman given poor materials to work with. At first he tries to get rid of them, but when he sees it is hopeless, he walks out, slamming the door, leaving everything to his assistant.

Pilots often find their instrument readings in conflict with their personal feelings. Although they may know that instruments do not usually lie, it is still not easy to discount one's own feelings as lies.

On Earth man need not ponder on which way is up, which way down. Such things are self-evident. Not so in space. Back in 1911 Tsiolkovskii contended that the state of weightlessness would alter the perception of surrounding space. He wrote:

> In a rocket there is no up or down, properly speaking, because there is no relative gravity, the ungrounded body does not rush toward the wall of

the rocket. But the subjective sense of up and down remains. We feel that there is an up and down but they shift with the shift in the direction of our body in space. Where our head is is up, where our feet are, down. Thus if we are turned headfirst toward Earth, it will appear to be up; if we are turned the other way Earth will seem below us in the abyss. The idea is grandiose and frightening the first time, then you grow accustomed to it and actually lose a sense of up and down.

The following experiment was done to test how well cosmonauts could orient themselves in a short period of weightlessness. The cosmonaut sat in the back seat of a two-seater jet plane strapped to his chair. On the part of the flight where weightlessness occurred, the pilot banked the plane at a 60° to 65° angle and the cosmonaut radioed out his sensations. It turned out that if his eyes were open, the cosmonaut could define his position without error; if his eyes were closed, he could not. No one was able to identify the maneuver the plane was making. Vladimir Komarov, for example, observed that "after the plane had banked, orientation in space was difficult. It seemed to me we were flying straight up."

Why did this happen? Man is informed of the relationship of his body to the plane of the Earth and of the relationship of objects to each other and to himself by the sensory organs—"the instruments of perception"—that respond to stimuli from the outside world (exteroceptors) and to stimuli from within the organism (interoceptors). The eyes, muscles, joints, skin, vestibular nerve all transmit information to the brain which is then capable of proper space perception.

One of the basic sensory organs involved in equilibrium, the vestibular nerve system, consists of the end organs, the conduction nerves, and the central nuclei in the medulla and the cells of the cortex. The end organs are in turn subdivided into the semicircular canals and the utricle of the inner ear. The three semicircular canals are filled with fluid, endolymph, and end in "brushes," the sensitive ends of the vestibular nerve.

In 1878 the St. Petersburg physiologist E. P. Tsion was the first to explain the significance of the semicircular canals in the formation of human perception of space. "The semicircular canals," he wrote, "are the end organs of spatial sense, that is to say, it is there that the irritation of the nerve ends serves to formulate our understanding of three-dimensional space."

The irritation mechanism is related to the laws of inertia. When the head is immobile or in a straight and even line with the body, the endolymph stays relatively immobile. But if the head turns or bends, the fluid in the semicircular canals flows to the side opposite the turn or bend. This irritates the vestibular nerve, which information is passed to the brain in the form of nerve impulses.

The utricle is essentially a gravity receptor, a device for transmitting information to the brain on a change in the force of gravity. The principle on which it works is fairly simple. The bottom of this small sac is covered with nerve cells and tiny hairs on which granulated calcium crystals lie in jellylike liquid. With a change in the force of gravity the crystals press on the vestibular nerve. The pressure of gravity changes with a rapid rise or fall, as anyone who has ever ridden an express elevator well knows.

The activity of the utricle in maintaining balance when the force of gravity changes was shown in the following experiment. Granulated crystals were removed from the utricle of a river crayfish and replaced with iron filings. The creature kept its proper spatial balance and swam as usual, spine up. But when the tester applied a magnet to the crayfish, it immediately changed position, responding to the force of the magnetic field. When the magnet was applied from above it turned spine down, when the magnet was applied from the side, the crayfish turned on its side.

The vestibular system is closely connected to the visual organs. If a man spins around in one place, then stops, the world for some time will seem to be spinning around him, because the visual organs also affect the vestibular nerve.

One experiment had a pilot watch a panoramic film while seated in a chair with an unsteady base. Before the film was shown, he was able to keep his chair balanced without losing his equilibrium. When the film began, showing a plane flying horizontally, the subject was relaxed, but when the plane banked and began making complicated maneuvers the subject rapidly lost his equilibrium and he and his chair collapsed to the floor. Along these same lines we know that on seeing a ship rolling in the waves on film, certain people become nauseated.

To test if the information from the semicircular canals is altered by weightlessness, a rotating chair was installed in the space laboratory. The cosmonaut was blindfolded and told to specify the angle of the tilt of the chair in which he was sitting. When the experiment was repeated under the condition of weightlessness, there were a great many more mistakes.

The force of Earth's gravity played a role not only in the formation of the skeleton and musculature of living creatures but in the development of the so-called proprioceptors (muscles, tendons, and joints). I. M. Sechenov has proved that no motor act can be completed with closed eyes without proprioceptive sensation, or in the language of cybernetics, without feedback. The muscle-joint complex which maintains the body in a certain position informs man of his position in relation to the surface of the Earth.

Touch is also an important source of information. When the body is in a vertical position, the nerve signals travel from the skin of the feet, in a horizontal position, from the spine, etc.

The receptors in the walls of the blood vessels and blood pressure are also indexes of the direction of the force of gravity. If a man is standing, let us say, the blood flowing downward creates greater pressure in the vessels of the lower extremities. That information goes directly to the brain.

Under the condition of weightlessness, not a single one of the sensory organs except the eyes gives full or accurate information on the position of the body in space. This is understandable: all the known receptors took their form as a response to Earth factors, whereas the eye took its form in response to the direct influence of space. S. I. Vavilov has figuratively called the human eye the "Sun" in the sense that it alone resulted from the effort of the organism to reach the Sun's rays so vitally important to it. It was visual sensations and perceptions that were the basis of the theoretical discovery of the universe, long before space flight.

Thus, with their eyes closed, cosmonauts were unable to estimate the position of the airplane correctly. Under the condition of weightlessness, the utricle either ceased transmitting information or, worse, supplied the brain with incorrect information. And then there were space illusions.

Space illusions

On a blind flight, at night, in the clouds, in a storm, a pilot cannot count on his eyesight, no matter how good it is. He can confuse a star for a ground light, ground lights for stars, a sloping bank of clouds for the horizon. Even more frequent are the illusions caused by banking, rotation, gliding in which it seems that the plane is flying upside-down.

In such situations the best advice a pilot can follow is not to believe his own eyes and to rely on his instruments, and only his instruments, which is not easy. He will literally have to hypnotize himself into believing that he is flying correctly. He must tell himself: The plane apparently heeled over but that can't

be because the instruments show no deviation whatever. So I must be wrong and the flight is taking a
normal course.

There is much food for illusion in space. When
Gherman Titov went weightless he felt as if he were
hanging upside-down, the instrument panel seemed
to be in the wrong place in the cabin—over his head—
but the illusion quickly disappeared, and the panel
went back to its proper place. Something similar happened to the American astronaut Gordon Cooper with
the onset of weightlessness. He thought he saw the
instrument bag near his right hand make a 90° turn.
But that illusion also disappeared when the astronaut
became accustomed to his new state.

What causes this type of illusion? Weightlessness
is preceded by acceleration stress. The spaceship ac-
celerates and the weight of the man forces him tight
to his chair. But the organism resists and the muscles
of the back pull away. Then weightlessness takes
place. The back muscles are still tensed by inertia,
giving the cosmonaut the false impression that he is
flying back down or head down. When the muscles
relax gradually, the switch to weightlessness does not
cause the same illusions.

The notion of up and down is worked out during
the training period on a mock-up spaceship. The cosmonaut is allowed to control the attitude of the
spacecraft with eyes open, then with windows closed,
then with eyes closed. Inside the cabin a man is usually guided not only by what he can see around him
but by simple touch, of the chair, the seat belt, the
instruments. He can cope with the information from
the utricle and get his proper bearings.

With their eyes opened, the majority of cosmonauts
were not troubled in their notion of up and down unless they saw starry sky "below" them and the surface
of the Earth "above," as proved by the following
experiment.

A rotating runner of a special material was fixed to
the wall of the space laboratory on which it was pos-

sible to walk in a condition simulating weightlessness. Walking the wall of that "pool" gave one the sensation of being not on a wall but on the floor, that "down" was underfoot. One had only to look through the window and see the surface of the Earth parallel to the body, and the sensation was destroyed.

But such erroneous information from the utricle can persist for a long period of time if the nervous system cannot stifle it.

In executing his various maneuvers the cosmonaut must have a clear idea of the attitude of the spacecraft vis-à-vis the Earth or some other objective in space, and a clear idea of what direction the craft is taking. Here is how Valerii Bykovskii got his bearings:

> When I switched over to manual controls, I started to look for Earth. I looked through the window and through the periscope and I could see a bit of the horizon. I realized that the right window was facing up, toward zenith. I moved the stick to the right and down. The side thruster didn't go off. The movement of the spacecraft became immediately apparent, I was working the three-axis control system on residual velocity. I thought, Fine, it'll be cheaper that way, and I waited. The movement of the Earth was just barely visible. We were running on residual velocity. I pushed the stick down and a side thruster didn't go off. But what was interesting was how well the spacecraft minded the manual control. I was overjoyed at how well things went. I found Earth through the periscope and landed the craft, having used up only 5 atmospheres.

Space illusions naturally interfere with maneuvers and can even lead to catastrophe. A flier was sent out on night assignment. On attaining altitude, he went into a cloud and immediately felt himself heeling over on the left. Not submitting to the sensation, he stuck to his flight plan but he was in torment, for the sensation did not disappear. When he started to land and could already see the airport, he felt that the plane was spiraling upward. The pilot became panicked. Making an incredible effort, he managed to land and emerged from the plane in a state of extreme nervous tension. His hands and legs were trembling and he could hardly walk. He was taken to the hospital where the diagnosis was grave. There could be no thought of his continuing work.

Special difficulties await the man who must transfer from one spacecraft to another any considerable distance away or who must make repairs on the spacecraft while in orbit. Tests were conducted in the space laboratory to find out how man could get his bearings in a state of weightlessness.

The cosmonauts were told to begin a transfer within the "weightlessness pool," close their eyes and continue estimating their position in space, then open their eyes and see how their estimates corresponded to the actual situation. It turned out that in the first two to five seconds after closing their eyes they could still estimate speed and rotation, although with some large errors. But it became more and more difficult. Nikolaev wrote in his report:

> In the first climb after shutting my eyes, I could still estimate my position in space by memory. While executing the transfer I felt in addition as if my body were rotating to the right. It was my impression that I must be somewhere in the middle of the pool and turned at a 75° to 90° angle. When I opened my eyes I saw I was in fact on the right side of the plane and turned at an angle of 180°, with my face to the ceiling.
>
> In the second climb I closed my eyes for approximately ten seconds. After four to six seconds I could no longer mentally picture my position in the pool. I had lost my bearings. When I opened my eyes I saw that I was by the tail of the plane with my head hanging down.

Estimating one's position on a space walk was just as difficult when the body rotated on a longitudinal axis. Popovich, for example, used the sound of the ventilator to get his bearings.

On a walk in space one no longer has the tactile and muscular sensations that give one one's bearings in the cabin. The cosmonaut has only the line that connects him to the spacecraft to give him his bearings. The information from his muscles, joints, and skin cannot tell him where he is, only of the interrelations between the various parts of his body. Thus he must rely mainly on his visual perceptions. And they are many. Here are Aleksei Leonov's impressions:

Opening the outer hatch of the Voskhod-2 you see before you the boundless universe in all its indescribable beauty. The Earth sailed past majestically looking quite flat, with only the curves at the edges to remind you that it was nonetheless a ball. Despite the rather thick glass of the window, I could see clouds, the glassy surface of the Black Sea, the shoreline, the range of the Caucasus, Novorossisk Bay. Going through the hatch, I felt a jolt, then the separation from the spacecraft. The line which was my connection to the spacecraft and my contact with the captain, slowly played out to its full length. The slight jolt had caused an insignificant change in the direction of the craft. Flying over the Earth, the spacecraft was bathed in the rays of the Sun. I observed no sharp contrasts of light and dark since the part of the spacecraft in shadow was lit by the reflection of the Sun's rays coming from Earth. Great green massifs, rivers, hills went swimming past—it was about like flying a plane at a high altitude. But because of the distance you couldn't make out cities or any relief details. It was like flying over an enormous colored map.

I had to keep moving about the spacecraft as we sped over the spinning Earth. I exited from the spacecraft with the back of my body at a 45° degree angle to the hatch, I returned headfirst with my hands outstretched to protect my head from hitting the hatch (or you can sprawl as in free fall on a parachute jump). I had to get my bearings from the moving ship or the "standing" Sun, which was over my head and behind me.

During training period back on Earth, a system for orientation in space on a space walk had been worked out for us. We had several dozen drawings of all the possible variants of the cosmonaut's position in open space to study. Also the weightless flights in a mock-up spacecraft in the space laboratory had psychologically strengthened the idea of the spacecraft being "underneath," and it was born out on the actual space walk.

On one of the walks my body went into a complicated twist as a result of the jolt from the spacecraft. The unblinking stars began to swim against the dark violet, then black velvet abyss of the sky. Then there would be just two stars in my field of vision, alternating with a view of the Earth and a view of the Sun. The Sun seemed to be hammered into the blackness of the sky. There was no way to stop my rotation. The line became twisted and my velocity dropped. Although I couldn't see the spacecraft during my rotation, I retained an image of its position and did not lose my bearings. My own position in space could be taken from the stars, the Sun, and the Earth. When it was fully extended, the line was another good guide.

So the orbital flights and the walk in space proved that even in these extraordinary conditions a man can get his bearings in space, by relying mainly on his vision.

But when spacecraft head for other planets and man by means of jet rockets can get farther and farther away from his spaceship out into open space, it is not impossible that there will be more space illusions. That is why cosmonauts are now being trained for their complicated duties under conditions close to those of interplanetary flight.

CHAPTER THREE

Without Ever Getting
off the Ground

What is most important in the training of fliers? Anyone who knows anything about aviation will say "flying." This is not to belittle the importance of theory, but as musicians say, in order to learn how to listen to music properly, you have to listen to music a lot.

Learning how to fly, the novice begins in a training plane equipped with dual controls, with an instructor who can come to his aid at any time. Unfortunately, at this time there are no practice space flights so the mock-up craft, in which situations that will be encountered in space can be simulated, assumes the most important role.

Teaching machines

In the age of cybernetics we have no small number of teaching machines, but for the moment the cosmonauts are not using them. The mock-ups are no less complex in their electronic equipment: they must re-create a space flight in every aspect—the movement of the craft, the workings of the various systems, the emergency situations—so that habitual skills can be worked out for every possible situation.

What is the advantage of habitual skill? First of all it allows a man to act quickly, automatically, without thinking in advance what he ought to do, what the consequences of the operation will be, and how each little thing must be carried out. An experienced pilot does not have to think about what must be done in order to gain altitude or to execute a certain maneuver because he has done it so many times that his automatic mechanism operates quickly and accurately.

But even the most habitual skill remains under conscious control; it is definitely not an involuntary action. No matter how habitual the operation, changes, deviations, disturbances, and errors are noticed immediately.

When mastering a new skill men rely on their past experience. They make comparisons, search for analogies, recall similar situations, and apply tried and true methods. Old habits can be serviceable in new situations, but sometimes they have to be changed. This is the first stage of ground training.

Ground-training devices or mock-ups are many and can be divided into the dynamic and the static—ones that move and others that are stationary. An example of a dynamic training device is the centrifuge, designed to teach the problems of control while under acceleration stress.

Ground-training devices can also be divided into categories according to the kind of skills they are trying to develop. Functional mock-ups are designed to teach general skills—how to work the various instruments or systems on the spacecraft, monitoring, radio transmission, etc.

Then there are specialized mock-ups designed to teach a man how to carry out special flight assignments—a walk in space, changing from one orbit to another, a rendezvous with another spacecraft or orbital stations. These mock-ups have only the systems and instruments the cosmonaut needs for a particular assignment.

All the proficiencies attained by the cosmonauts on the functional and specialized mock-ups are then tested on a more complex mock-up, the first of which was the practice craft Vostok. This was an actual model of the spacecraft equipped to simulate the movement of the Earth and stars and all aspects of the flight: blast-off, orbit, and landing. It had a place for the instructor, electrocardiograph equipment, computer, instrument panel, manual controls, atmospheric control system, radio transmitters—everything exactly as it would be on an actual Vostok spacecraft.

Working on the practice craft, the cosmonauts became acquainted with the capsule and its equipment. They learned the normal workings and possible deviations of all the systems. They learned to master the manual controls, the radio system, the atmospheric control system, how to conduct scientific experiments, how to fill in the flight log. They learned what to do in an emergency situation.

The final stage of training was a test "flight" simulating all conditions, including time, of an actual space flight as closely as possible (with the exception of acceleration stress and weightlessness). The simulated flights followed a set pattern. A general assignment was made, then specified, and the flight log was filled out. The cosmonaut donned his space suit, formally declared his readiness, and entered the spacecraft. Seated in the capsule, he switched on the radio transmission and checked out his equipment. Having completed the check he would make his report on the equipment, his own feelings, his readiness to begin. Then powerful amplifiers would simulate the blast-off of the booster rockets, gradually bringing up the noise of the jet engines. Once the cosmonaut had "gone into orbit" and was carrying out his assignment, he would make additional reports on the tape recorder.

The simulated flights gradually became more complex. First there was just a one-orbital flight. Then there was practice in an emergency situation and manually controlled landing.

As he worked the cosmonaut would report on his own mistakes. Then the instructor would comment. The final grade would depend on the quantity and character of the mistakes made. A cosmonaut might get an "unsatisfactory" for just one mistake if it was one that would have led to catastrophe in a real situation: if, for example, he fired the retro-rockets when the craft was not pointing in the proper direction.

The final evaluation of a cosmonaut's work took many factors into consideration: his work tempo, his emotional state, the character of his mistakes, his ability to evaluate himself and recognize his inaccuracies and blunders, the quality of his reports. For maximum objectivity the grade was given only after consultation between instructors and doctors.

The simulated flights gave the cosmonauts firsthand experience for a real flight and worked out the general rules for the development of professional skills, as well uncovering the individual idiosyncrasies of the cosmonauts in training.

Learning from mistakes

"To err is human" and the cosmonauts were no exception. They all made mistakes, but mistakes that diminished in number and gradually disappeared. The most frequent mistakes (30%) were made in the radio reports. Preoccupied with their assignments, cosmonauts seldom or never reported on their instrument readings, the stage of the rockets, their own feelings about the flight, about leaving the dark side of the Earth, about the progress of their work, about the light signals. But one of the most important factors in a space flight is the accuracy of the information passing between the spacecraft and the tracking stations.

We have already said that radio transmissions by UHF were limited to the time when the spacecraft was passing over the U.S.S.R. The cosmonauts generally employed standard jargon in their exchanges with the tracking stations, but of course not all exchanges could be foreseen. Titov reported:

> The one time they didn't understand me on Earth was not the transmitter's fault. The Far East tracking station was playing a waltz, "Amur Waves," on the short wave. I love that waltz and when the boys in the tracking station asked, "That bothering you or do you like it?" I said, "Thanks, sure I

do." So the Far East station began playing it again. Then again and again. I interrupted, "Thanks boys, change the record." "Roger," was the answer. And after a minute, "Amur Waves" again. That was some Roger!

No less comic was an incident on Vostok-5. On that five-day flight Bykovskii radioed something about his "first chair in space." The tracking station picked up "first flare in space." Naturally everyone got excited: had the flare been a collision with a meteorite? It was almost an hour before they made radio contact again and Bykovskii was told to report immediately where and when he'd seen the flare, what it had been like, what was the pressure in the cabin, etc.

Information can also be distorted by typographical error. During the Vostok-4 flight the tracking station transmitted an order for what should have been Descent 3 as Descent 111. "That threw me off at first," Popovich reported, "but then I figured it out. The typewritten order had been in roman numerals—III— but the comrade transmitting it read it as arabic numerals."

Even accurately received information of nonstandard character can lead to false conclusions. A cosmonaut undergoing an extended experiment in an isolation chamber had an unscheduled talk late one Sunday night with a fellow cosmonaut, Sergei Pavlovich Korolov. That day Andrian Nikolaev and Valentina Tereshkova had been married in town and Korolov had been invited. The subject knew nothing about the wedding; as a condition of the experiment he was to receive no information whatever in the isolation chamber. When Korolov dropped in and learned that one of his fellow cosmonauts was in the isolation chamber, he took up the microphone. The chief medic turned it on and told the subject that Korolov wanted to talk with him, and he answered that he was happy to talk but he would prefer that it not be from the isolation chamber. Korolov congratulated him on how well the experiment was going and hoped that it would finish as well. The cosmonaut thanked Korolov and there the conversation ended.

The information received by the cosmonaut in isolation had contained no false data, but it was completely misconstrued. In his report later the cosmonaut wrote, "The conversation set me thinking. In the first place, it's Sunday, in the second place Sunday evening and Korolov suddenly appears outside the isolation chamber. When the mike went on, I thought they must be letting me out. Then when I heard Sergei Pavlovich I thought they can't be letting me out, just telling me something. But why is he here? I had this strange idea that there must be some urgent unscheduled mission if Korolov was there on a Sunday evening to discuss it."

The misconstrued information had an emotional effect on the cosmonaut that was reflected in the progress of the experiment right up to the end. Ignorance of the events in town combined with the chance conversation with Korolov on a day off led the cosmonaut to the most subjectively probable conclusion relating to his professional interests. He never considered the real reason for Korolov's visit as it was from his point of view improbable and irrelevant.

There were many mistakes made at first by the cosmonauts in monitoring the instruments, working the manual controls, and using the Earth path indicator. This was because the manual controls of a spacecraft differ significantly from airplane controls and the spinning globe was altogether a new instrument. But nonetheless the cosmonauts mastered the new secrets of their profession with comparative ease because there were earlier mastered skills involved. A tractor driver will learn to drive a tank faster than a locksmith, a locksmith will be able to repair one better than a teacher. There is a transfer of skills thanks to which a driver who has driven various kinds of machines can quickly master an unfamiliar one, a test pilot familiar with various types of planes can cope with a totally new model, and a man who knows several languages can master another without difficulty.

The Vostok cosmonauts, with the exception of Tereshkova, had already flown jet planes and other aircraft, and the professional skills learned in the air —the ability to divide one's attention properly, or to estimate one's position in space correctly—helped them adapt fairly quickly to the spacecraft. For the women cosmonauts with an insufficiently developed spatial sense, due to a lack of flying experience, there were supplementary exercises at the manual controls. Within four to eight test flights the number of errors had been cut in half.

In order to be corrected an error must be noticed as quickly as possible. This is the reason that in target shooting the target is called after every shot, not after a series, so the marksman can adjust his aim immediately.

Understanding of error is one of the most important conditions in the successful formation of skills. On the test flights it was the instructor who called the errors, but much attention was devoted to getting the cosmonaut himself to recognize the strengths and weaknesses in his work, to find the reasons for the latter and the means for correcting them. Such self-control is not learned all at once, it comes with experience. At first the cosmonauts did not take notice of errors or failures to follow instructions, they lacked control over their work. But gradually they perfected their control and began noticing not only gross errors but even minor ones not always caught even by the instructor.

In the meantime the spacecraft systems were being changed. The flight plans became more complex and the instruments were perfected, requiring the acquisition of new skills. The number of errors would go up again. Originally the cosmonauts had to turn on the oxygen feed to the space suit themselves. Later, when the feed system was changed, they went on turning it on according to the old habit. One could cite many examples, all attesting to the importance of changing the spacecraft construction as little as possible on the one hand, and of constant acquisition of new skills on the other.

Pavlov showed that it is the central nervous system that gives functions their strength. A well-learned skill is a "dynamic stereotype" whose strength is its very inertia. But it can interfere with the development of new skills in a changed situation. In other words, the stronger the skill, the harder it is to replace it. This is something of a contradiction. The cosmonauts work to develop solid skills, only to have the engineers constantly perfecting the spacecraft, rendering many of those skills obsolete. Komarov for example had to learn certain skills three times over. As backup man for Popovich he perfected control of Vostok. Then in preparation for the Voskhod flight there were a few things he had to relearn. The third time was the flight of Soyuz-1 which in its construction was essentially different from preceding spacecraft and required a new set of handling skills. On both those flights, it must be said, Komarov performed brilliantly.

The experience of training cosmonauts has shown that skills must be supple and based on a conscious understanding of the operation, not on a simple mechanical reflex. In order that they be supple, the idiosyncrasies of character and temperament of each man must be known.

Going back to Hippocrates

The Greek physician Hippocrates (460–377 B.C.), considered the father of medicine, found in the endless variety of human behavior certain common traits permitting a division of men into basic types according to temperament. Having repudiated magic and sorcery, working from empirical knowledge, he asserted that according to the laws of nature, (1) the brain was the thinking organ, and (2) the doctor must treat not the sickness but the patient, giving thought to his individual characteristics and environment. Many of Hippocrates' views have been confirmed and developed in our time.

Hippocrates sought the cause of illness and of differences in character among men in the material processes and phenomena of the organism. He explained differences of character by a predominance of one or another humor: in the sanguine it was blood manufactured by the heart; in the phlegmatic it was phlegm formed in the brain; in the choleric, the yellow bile of the liver; in the melancholic, the black bile of the spleen.

This explanation of temperament seems very naive today. But the central idea of a connection between personality types and biological characteristics is correct. In studying the physiology of the brain, Pavlov established that temperament depends on the type of nervous system. According to Pavlov, excitation and inhibition are the basic processes of the nervous system and they can be characterized by their strength, equilibrium, and mobility. The strength of the nerve processes is an index of the capacity of the nerve cells and of the nervous system as a whole. A strong nervous system can sustain a burden that would make a weak one break down. Nerve processes are not always balanced, sometimes one is stronger than another; equilibrium is the balance between impulse and reflex. Mobility is the speed of change from one process to another.

Pavlov emphasized that the basic processes of the nervous system could come together in various combinations, but that Hippocrates had correctly pointed to the four most characteristic: "We have taken our four types from Hippocrates—the weak correspond to the melancholic, the strong, unequilibrated (excitable) to the choleric, the strong, equilibrated to the phlegmatic and to the sanguine."

How does Pavlov define temperament? "Temperament is the general character of a man, the basic character of his nervous system which puts its stamp on all the individual's activities."

How does temperament affect the cosmonaut's activities? The question has been extensively researched. Specifically, it affects how quickly the cosmonaut masters a problem, whether or not he repeats one type of error during training, how quickly he masters control skills in ordinary circumstances and special circumstances, how he is affected by work interruptions, how critical he is of his own performance. At work and at play the cosmonauts were studied and it was discovered that each man's nervous system had a great deal to do with his mastery of operational skills on board the spacecraft.

Let us say then that the unequilibrated temperament corresponds to the choleric type. "The choleric type," writes Pavlov, "is clearly aggressive, energetic, quickly and easily excited." The choleric type tends to be cyclical in his activities and his emotions. He is capable of giving himself to something with all his might, getting carried away in a surge or emotion, he is eager to overcome and does overcome any difficulties and obstacles in his path. But then his strength is exhausted, he goes into a slump, "he becomes excessively exhausted, he overworks himself to the point where he can no longer stand it."

The choleric type is impetuous, highly irritable, irascible, sharp in his relationships, straightforward, highly tense in all his activities.

Working out his classification of nervous types, Pavlov put himself in the choleric class. "I am an excitable type," he wrote, "my inhibitory processes are poor. It is hard for me to wait for any length of time for example; it is a variation of the same response that is expressed in my nervousness, suspiciousness, etc." From among the famous in history, Pavlov put Peter I, Pushkin, Suvorov, and Chapaev in the same category.

The cosmonauts in the choleric category were quick to master their professional skills. But they made many mistakes at the beginning of training, in their tendency to get ahead of things. They were better at mastering special assignments, including special flight assignments, than ordinary ones. During the preliminary discussions they asked a lot of questions and took a great interest in the details of the assignment. On the practice craft they worked quickly, with initiative, reacting to everything emotionally. Their typical mistakes were a result of haste and insufficient concentration. Their reports were clear, lively, picturesque, but at times insufficiently concrete and rather subjective.

Leonov, of whom we will speak later, is a clear example of this type. Titov too has this kind of temperament. He quickly mastered the controls and the few mistakes he made were made in haste. Later when the skills were mastered he worked happily, with initiative and without error. His reports were outstanding for their interest, clarity, profound self-evaluations, and fullness.

The strong, equilibrated type with mobile nerve processes corresponds to the sanguine type. According to Pavlov's definition the sanguine type "is a fervent, very productive worker but only when there is much that is interesting to be done, that is, when he is in a state of constant excitement." The sanguine type is agile, and adapts to changing life conditions; he makes contact quickly with those around him; he is sociable and feels no constraint with new people. In a group he is gay and joyful; he takes up new projects eagerly and is capable of getting carried away. His feelings are easily aroused and easily changed. He can conquer fear in a dangerous situation. He is generally optimistic.

The great agility of the nervous processes renders the mind of the sanguine type supple, so that he can switch his attention from one thing to another.

Herzen, Lermontov, Frunze, and Makarov were typical sanguine types. As was Gagarin. The clinical psychological report on Gagarin made before his first flight says:

All during the training and testing period Yuri Gagarin did very well in the various psychological experiments. He was unflustered by strong sudden stimuli. His reactions to new situations (the state of weightlessness, prolonged isolation in the isolation chamber, parachute jumping) were always positive: there was rapid orientation and ability to handle himself in various unexpected situations.

In isolation chamber he showed a well-developed ability to relax, even in the brief rest periods, to go to sleep quickly, and to wake up at a given time.

Another characteristic that might be mentioned is his sense of humor, his good-natured and joking disposition.

During the simulated flights on the practice spacecraft his characteristic style of work was calm and sure, and the delivery of his reports afterward was clear and concise. His mastery of his professional skills was marked by a unique confidence, thoughtfulness, curiosity, and cheerfulness.

The person in whom nerve processes of excitation and inhibition are fairly equilibrated and comparatively immobile belongs to the phlegmatic type. According to Pavlov, "The phlegmatic type is one of life's calm, even-tempered, steady, persistent toilers. Thanks to the equilibrium of the nervous processes and a certain inertia, the phlegmatic type stays calm even in difficult situations. The equilibrium between excitation and inhibition makes it easy for him to keep his temper. He will not be distracted by trifles and can therefore carry out a job requiring a steady expense of strength, a prolonged and methodical effort." Krylov and Kutuzov exhibited such traits.

The cosmonauts of this type mastered things more slowly, repeatedly making one kind of mistake. They acted first, then reported, without noticing their mistakes. An ordinary flight assignment was easier for them than something special. During the early stages of training they asked few questions but they were essential questions, to clarify important details. They worked calmly, accurately, unhurriedly, and their reports were objective, detailed, and systematic, but standard. Cosmonauts of this type made steady improvement and steadily fewer mistakes. They paid practically no attention to interruptions.

Nikolaev is of a phlegmatic temperament. Given the relatively high immobility and strength of his nerve processes, his mastery of skills was comparatively slow. His mistakes were many, but of only one type, and they gradually disappeared. An ordinary flight exercise he mastered quickly. His work during the training period was characterized by deliberation, concentration, accuracy, and great emotional self-control. His reports were clear and concise. It was a certain purposefulness, keenness of observation, seriousness, and ability to generalize that gave him his reputation as the wise one among the cosmonauts.

People of the melancholic type are usually shy, indecisive, timid. They are frightened by new situations, new people; they become confused and lost in their associations with people and tend to keep to themselves. Gogol and Tchaikovsky were representatives of this type.

Smart or dumb, honest or dishonest, good or evil, talented or untalented, a man has some kind of temperament, as the psychologist Platonov observed. People with a weak nervous system, melancholics, cannot be cosmonauts since cosmonauts must work to the limits of their physical and psychic potentialities. But the participation of melancholics as scientific advisers and specialists cannot be completely ruled out.

Psychological analysis of skill mastery on a practice spacecraft shows that the process depends on the individual character of the cosmonaut. Men with differing types of nervous systems can attain the same high level of achievement, although their paths to mastery may be different. A well-learned skill is a well-learned skill regardless of the speed of mastery or number of mistakes during training.

Crucible in space

The unusual phenomena man must expect on a spacecraft—acceleration stress and weightlessness—unfortunately cannot be simulated simultaneously on a practice craft. But they can be simulated separately in the centrifuge, aircraft, heat chambers, altitude and isolation chambers.

In actual space flight these phenomena are not separate but consecutive (acceleration stress changes to weightlessness) or simultaneous (nervous tension, isolation, radiation effect coming all at once). So the cosmonaut must be able to coordinate all his acquired skills. This is the real test of his knowledge, experience, and ability.

Once in orbit, a cosmonaut has to be able to observe, maintain radio contact, sustain the shift from acceleration stress to weightlessness (during which he cannot lose control), eat, take pictures, make experiments—carry out the program.

Here is Popovich on his flight:

> I got the attitude of the craft under control without any special difficulty and tried to see what I could see on the surface of the Earth. The manual control worked fine. I was able to fix things in place and observe them through the central section of the periscope.
>
> My next job was to control the attitude of the craft on the dark side of the Earth lighted only by the Moon. I controlled the direction by using the clouds. A cloud through the central part of the periscope has a grayish color but is white through the outer ring.
>
> Studying the clouds I could even see which way they were going because of their density and visibility against the black Earth.
>
> I was pretty successful at keeping focused on the stars which will be so important in future work in astronomy. Having found my constellation I'd choose a bright star and watch it through the inner ring of the periscope. As I watched I would see it moving down toward the center. As soon as it

reached the center I would manipulate the manual control until it was right in the center. I came to the conclusion that you could not only control the craft by the stars but also make astronomical observations.

A mock-up craft is different from a real one. The equipment may be the same, the flight dynamics accurately reproduced, the radio transmission, the emergency situations, the general living and working conditions all quite accurately reproduced. But an imitation is never identical with reality. As in all models the craft controls are simplified, schematized. On an actual flight the cosmonaut must bring the skills learned on the mock-up into line with his perceptions of space and the actual behavior of an actual craft. A skill too rigidly learned in training may not be desirable.

Titov, Nikolaev, Popovich, and Bykovskii were able to control the craft manually thanks to their experience as fighter pilots. They already knew how to apply skills learned in training to an actual flight and on the mock-ups were able to "play with" all the possible deviations they might encounter. Their skills, in other words, were realistically structured, not rigidly programed.

Speaking of the value of flying experience Belyaev emphasized that "control of the spacecraft is not especially difficult, especially if a man has had flying experience, even though piloting a plane and controlling a spacecraft are not the same."

There is also the possibility that certain skills may not be learned rigidly enough. On long interplanetary flights cosmonauts run the risk of forgetting their training. Therefore it will be necessary to equip interplanetary craft with special training devices that will enable the cosmonauts to keep up their skills.

Vostok-1 was designed for one man. When Voskhod-1 and Voskhod-2 were about to go into orbit, a new problem arose—team training for multimanned spacecraft.

CHAPTER FOUR

The Team on an Interplanetary Craft

The flight of the multimanned Vostok was a qualitatively new step in the conquest of space. Multimanned spacecraft fired by fuel rockets or nuclear energy will be making flights to the Moon and to planets. The dream of mankind has moved surely from the pages of science fiction to the drawing boards of scientists and now resides in figures, calculations, experiments conducted on Earth and in orbital flights. The trajectories are being plotted, schedules and supplies are being figured out.

We know that a spacecraft moving on a semielliptical trajectory at an initial speed of 100 miles per second will take 260 days to get to Mars. Rather a long period of time, creating a number of problems. The spacecraft "population" will have to keep watch on the controls around the clock, as Earth understands the term; they will have to maintain radio contact, study navigation, conduct experiments and make reports, monitor all systems and instruments and if necessary repair them. After landing on an unknown planet no end of work awaits them.

Space on a spacecraft is limited. Every gram of weight must be counted and, just as important, the space assigned to life-support systems supplying normal air and food must be regulated. Is the answer to increase the size of the spacecraft? That will depend on the productivity of the closed ecological system which will in turn depend on the freight capacity of the rockets. Reducing the number of cosmonauts on board would jeopardize the whole project. Another solution must be found, and in our opinion it is in the broadest possible training of cosmonauts.

Space brigade

Many years of sailing experience have testified to the fact that the enforced cooperation of different professions is not a utopian situation. The teams of the first interplanetary craft may well be made up of from four to six such men.

Who will be included on these expeditions? In the first place, a captain—an experienced cosmonaut with aeronautic and engineering training. He must know navigation, radio transmission, the structure of the basic systems, and the spacecraft in general. He will be in command of the men and take over the controls during the crucial and complex periods of the flight, such as blast-off and landing.

No ship or aircraft can get along without a navigator. This cosmonaut will have to know cosmology (a branch of astronomy dealing with the general structure of the universe) and space navigation. He will be the one to work out the best trajectory for the flight and the means of getting the spacecraft into that trajectory.

When other planets become points of departure and arrival the spacecraft will be moving within their gravitational field and the parameters of its trajectory will depend on the character and mass of the planets. Besides determining the spacecraft's position, the navigator will also determine the directional flow of meteorites in order to avoid collision. The navigator must know not only the structure of the universe through which the spacecraft is passing, but also about the destination planet—the acceleration of gravity on its surface, composition of the atmosphere, condition of the terrain, soil structure, etc. Possibly he will have to act as meteorologist, geodesist, and seismologist. In certain situations he must be ready to take over as captain.

No interplanetary flight can get along without a radio engineer. He will keep in communication with Earth, locate by radar any meteorites about to collide with the spacecraft, and estimate the exact landing distance. In addition, he will keep track of radioactivity in the space around the spacecraft. He will be broadly informed about the destination planet and be able to conduct experiments there.

There will probably be one or two engineers responsible for the workings of the various spacecraft systems. And there will be a doctor on the team.

Voskhod-1 had a doctor on board in addition to a medical supply unit well stocked with medicines. Dr. Boris Egorov took blood pressures of himself and his comrades, drew blood for blood tests, trapped exhaled air for analysis, tested the sensitivity of nervous systems, tested eyes for color discrimination, kept track of organic functional changes, and studied the effect of weightlessness on the working efficiency and psychic state of the crew.

The cosmonaut doctor will be specially trained for long space flights. He too must become a universal man. He will keep track of the health of the members of the team and be in charge of the atmospheric control system. On the destination planet he will be zoologist, botanist, microbiologist and will make chemical analyses of air and soil. If the need arises the cosmonaut doctor must be able to perform as a surgeon. Other members of the team will have to assume the roles of nurses and assistants.

All members of the space team must be able to assume each other's roles. Each must be able to monitor the controls. Possibly all members of the team will be needed simultaneously during blast-off, rendezvous or landing, passing through a dangerous spatial zone, high radiation zone, or meteorite shower zone.

We have already talked of the one-man spacecraft as a complicated link between man and machine. The multimanned spacecraft with its links between man and man and machine will be much more complicated. While the relatively narrow specialization and division of labor on a multimanned spacecraft permits more control than on the one-man craft where everything lies on the shoulders of one man, division of labor demands absolute coordination of activities, profound mutual understanding among the members of the team, and the ability to take over each other's work.

Harmony of the group is especially important in situations where decisions must be reached quickly, when there is no time for reflection. Contemporary aviation experience has shown that even when all the members of a team know what they must do, there must also be psychological compatibility between the members to achieve the degree of harmony required in a time-deficit situation. Otherwise it won't be achieved, even with the pilot, navigator, radio engineer all separately acting correctly.

G. I. Kalashnik, a flying instructor and recipient of the medal of Hero of Socialist Labor, has written:

> Experience has shown that when the professional training and discipline of each member is supported by mutual assistance and cooperation, you get results.
>
> The pilot, radio engineer, mechanic, and navigator must each know his job to perfection. But they all must also know that they have an obligation to their comrades on the team, and be ready to back them up.
>
> I remember dozens of examples where a lack of mutual assistance, trust, and solidarity among members of a team led to terrible accidents.
>
> In a complicated situation (bad weather conditions, a breakdown of some sort) the team must stand fast. It is a bad situation if each one "does his own thing," relying only on the captain for orders.
>
> An emergency situation must not take a team unawares. They must not be caught napping, and must be able to become as one. Assurance of course comes with years; only prolonged work together permits a knowledge of each other's capacities.

At first glance one might be tempted to explain team disharmony in terms of lack of friendship or mutual respect, or even in terms of dislike. But in fact, the main cause of disharmony is lack of prolonged cooperation in an actual flying situation.

An experienced commander will always pay attention to the psychological propensities of the members of his team and change the crew around if necessary. It is a well-known fact of the Second World War that the American air force suffered serious losses until psychologists recommended that flight teams be assigned in accord with the results of psychological tests.

It would seem that putting together a team is not difficult—one simply calls in the specialists, administers the psychological tests, and sends the men into training. But it is not enough just to find an amicable team. A group made up entirely of "sports-star" types, for example, though amicable and cohesive, is a weak team.

Even when we know the temperaments of the individuals, it is impossible to predict how a group will behave as a whole, what kinds of relations will develop between individuals, how the activities of any given individual will accord with those of the collective. A group is not a mathematical sum of individuals but an organism in itself, with its own laws. Group harmony on a regular flying team is achieved with repeated flights, and if it is not achieved, the group can be changed. Since there will be no such change during a long space flight, psychologists must be able to select and train a harmonious team in advance.

Group psychology

Space psychologists are not the only ones interested in group harmony. It has drawn the attention of industrial managers, sports coaches, military leaders—everyone in charge of a group of people with a job to do.

Back in the thirties in our Institute for the Protection of Labor, research was begun on the rational organization of men in labor and industry. A study was made of a group assembling small articles on an assembly line. Interesting general rules became apparent. The individuals in the group had not been specially selected so one would expect a slow work tempo, with the faster workers being held back by the slower. But it turned out that the group's tempo was higher than that of the average worker. The tempo, it developed, depended on the positioning of the workers. When a fast worker was seated next to a slow one on the line the tempo picked up; an opposite arrangement led to an opposite result.

The importance of team selection is vividly illustrated by experiences with sports teams. Today's level of achievement in sports has been made possible by attention paid to psychic-physiological factors, to the problem of cohesiveness, of mutual understanding between the individual players which has given maximum effectiveness to the group as a whole.

The famous Brazilian soccer player Pele, in answer to reporters' questions, said that in his opinion his young teammate Kutino was an "ideal" player because he knew how to guess the play Pele was going to make.

The Soviet scholar M. A. Novikov has proved that "leaders" and "followers" will emerge in any isolated group. The leader is the one who imposes his will on the others, who defines the tactic (line of behavior) of the group as a whole. In sports, the leader either actively takes the ball or directs the play of his teammates.

Leadership is not a permanent role; it is a role taken by a man in a certain situation. The ship's captain is leader so long as he stands on the bridge; he may become a follower down below where one of the crew has assumed the role of leader. Nor can it be assumed that the leader is the best member of the group, the followers second-class members. An orchestra must have a conductor and musicians. There cannot be good leaders and bad followers, since the group is a complex mechanism in which all roles are necessary and important.

A group of scientists working under Professor Gorbov studying the problems of group psychology have proposed a series of methods for determining how successful the activities of a given group will be. Their method is the so-called "homeostatic method." Interestingly, it has as its basis observations Gorbov made in a mental institution.

In this institution there were four shower stalls served by a water pipe of such size that it could not provide all four with a sufficient quantity of hot water. When all four stalls were occupied, only one would get hot water and the other stalls would get cold. Before long a scheme acceptable to all was worked out because one individual quickly assumed control—became the leader. It would have taken the group much longer to work things out if two or three men had aspired to leadership. The members of the group might have gone on interfering with each other and never have settled the matter of the showers. It is a hopeless situation unless there is someone in the group willing to set himself apart from the others.

An analogous situation was set up with an instrument called the "homeostat." Each member of the group could change the position of the arrows not only of his own instrument but the others'. The subjects were told to set all arrows on the gauges at a certain number (zero, for example) but of course they kept interfering with each other, and were able to solve the problem only when one of them took the initiative and made himself leader while the rest automatically submitted to his authority.

The results of many similar experiments were useful in the formation of the first space teams. Three tough men trained for the first Voskhod flight, each one an expert in his field. The methodologists, psychologists, and instructors were most interested in how well the team could cooperate. They were studied on test flights, in sports tests, at work and at play.

Special training was required for Feoktistov, a scientist, and Egorov, a doctor, who had not had the flying training Komarov had had. They had to master the art of radio transmission and learn to operate the environmental control system, etc. Special training was followed by group training which gave each member of the team the chance to know and evaluate the others and to figure out the best way to integrate his activities with theirs.

Spacecraft captain Komarov was a man who worked with deliberation and calm, and could make systematic, full, objective, and self-critical reports afterward. A superb flier, he proved a brilliant leader who could tactfully but firmly organize a group for the completion of a task.

Feoktistov showed initiative and clear thinking in every training test. He was observant, and given to studying every assignment in detail, often coming up with new answers to what had been considered settled and uninteresting questions.

Egorov was characteristically thorough, persistent, self-critical, and capable of intelligent initiative.

Komarov wrote of the successful Voskhod-1 flight:

> The team managed to carry out the whole research program as planned during the one day. The efforts of the whole team were required. One man couldn't have done it, no matter how well he'd been trained. It required not only identical understanding of the job by all members of the team but cooperation. We had to be quick on the uptake and interchangeable.
>
> Our space team was a small but amicable group proud in the knowledge that we were working for universal goals, for the good of all mankind.
>
> Each member of the team helped the others in the complex and interesting work, and we did it, but it wasn't easy. Before ever getting in Voskhod's cabin, the team had worked hard, studied hard, trained hard.

Komarov defined his own role as captain with characteristic modesty: "It must be explained that the captain of a spacecraft is not the same as the captain of an army division. No orders were given, none were required. We all knew what we had to do and we did it."

The Voshkod-2 flight required even greater cooperation and harmony since so complex an assignment as a walk in space could only be accomplished with the fullest mutual understanding, trust, and confidence. The team assignment was made according to both professional (Belyaev and Leonov were both highly qualified pilots) and psychological criteria.

Belyaev is a man of great willpower and self-control even in the most dangerous situations, with a logical mind capable of profound self-analysis, and great persistence in the face of difficulties.

Leonov by temperament belongs to the choleric type. Strong and impetuous, he is capable of furious activity showing decisiveness and daring. Artistically gifted, he can reproduce a picture accurately after only brief study.

These two temperamentally different men complemented one another to make an excellent team that carried out a difficult program successfully. They both had been trained as no men ever before to work in the bottomless vacuum of space. Leonov's walk in space and return to the cabin had been simulated on a mock-up to work out the operation of all systems involved. What the captain ought to do in an emergency situation during a space walk was carefully worked out. Afterward Belyaev and Leonov went right on talking, so important to them was the harmony they'd achieved on the mock-up exercise.

But mere coordination of activities in controlling the spacecraft and its systems does not exhaust the problem. On long space flights men will have to live together in prolonged isolation. The decisive factor will be the relationships among the members of the

team, the sympathy, the shared point of view that
creates solidarity.

Friendship

Aristotle said that "friendship is the most necessary
thing in life." It is friendship, not "efficient relations,"
that makes for success on a long space flight.

The history of expeditions does not lack sad examples of trouble between people working together over
a long period of time. One telling episode is from the
life of the great Norwegian arctic explorer Fridtjof
Nansen. Leaving their ship *Fram* drifting along the
84th latitude, Nansen and Johansen set out on skis
for the North Pole. Having reached a latitude of
86° 14′ and seeing the uselessness of going on, they
turned back south. After almost a year and a half
they reached Franz Josef Land. Through the ice and
wet they walked in their permanently frozen clothes.
Half starved, they ate walrus and polar bear, and
drank snow that had been melted in flasks held next
to their bodies. Nansen hurt his arm. But the worst
of all their sufferings was the relationship between
them. They seldom talked to one another, sometimes
not for a week at a time, and when they did, they
were official in tone. Johansen, for example, never
called Nansen anything but "Monsieur Chief of
Expedition."

We know from everyday experience that though
we may be able to work with some people we would
not necessarily choose them as companions on a
holiday or even a trip to the movies, because then we
usually choose someone we find interesting or pleasant.

But we also know of many cases where the difficult
circumstances surrounding the expedition have co-
alesced the collective. Arctic explorers have been able
to work together for as long as nine months at a time.
Friendship helped Thor Heyerdahl's men cross the

Pacific on the *Kon-Tiki* in the most dangerous, nearly tragic conditions.

Early in 1960 a storm in the Pacific drove a barge away from the Kuril Islands out into the ocean, carrying four Soviet soldiers, Askhat Zigashin, Filipp Poplavskii, Anatolii Kriuchkovskii, and Ivan Fedotov. After drifting for 49 days, they were picked up by an American aircraft carrier and taken to San Francisco. It had been an amazing feat, but what most surprised the foreign correspondents was the sense of solidarity among the soldiers. Here is an excerpt from an interview:

REPORTER: I know that in such circumstances it is possible for men to lose their humanity, to go out of their minds, turn into animals. You must have had fights, fistfights even, over the last piece of bread or the last drop of water?

ZIGASHIN: For the entire 49 days none of us exchanged a single nasty word. When the fresh water began to run out, we each got half a cup a day. No one took an extra drop. On Anatolii Kriuchkovskii's birthday we offered him double, but he refused.

REPORTER: You celebrated your friend's birthday under such hellish circumstances? Did you think about death, Mr. Zigashin?

ZIGASHIN: No, we thought we were too young to give up easily.

REPORTER: What did you do during all those long days? You, for example, Mr. Poplavskii?

POPLAVSKII: We made fishhooks out of tin cans, we unbraided rope to make fishline. Askhat repaired the lantern. Sometimes I read aloud.

REPORTER: What was the name of the book?

POPLAVSKII: *Martin Eden*, by Jack London.

REPORTER: Incredible!

FEDOTOV: Sometimes Filipp would play the accordion and we'd sing.

REPORTER: Let's see this accordion.

FEDOTOV: We ate it, unfortunately.

REPORTER: What? How?

FEDOTOV: It was simple. The leather parts we

cut into strips and boiled in sea water. It turned
out to be sheepskin so we used to say we had
two grades of meat: prime, from the accordion,
second grade, our shoes.

REPORTER: It's unbelievable you had strength
enough for jokes. Do you know yourselves the kind
of people you are?

ZIGASHIN: Ordinary Soviet people.

Even though it is undoubtedly an easier task to put
together a space team in this country than in capi-
talist countries since we are taught from infancy to be
collective in spirit, men still maintain their individual-
ity and reveal themselves differently in different small-
group situations.

One experiment which lasted 120 days in a pressurized cabin simulating the conditions in space was
a complete success with a spirit of collectivism, co-
hesion, and mutual support that overcame problems
and helped the men live and work together amicably
for the entire period.

But another experiment lasting only 70 days pre-
sented a very different picture. This was an experiment in which Dr. Stanislav Bugrov, engineer Leonard
Smirichevskii, and radio correspondent Evgenii Tereshchenko took part and they all kept diaries. It was
soon clear that the doctor and the engineer were
psychologically incompatible. During their leisure
hours they were constantly in conflict. When the experiment was over the subjects reported that the
psychological incompatibility had had an adverse
effect on all three. Here are some excerpts from
Tereshchenko's diary that give an insight into that
isolated world. Three weeks after the beginning of
the experiment he wrote:

> Watch, dinner, medical tests, sleep. Our life has fall-
> en into a feverish monotonous pattern. We have al-
> most no free time. We're beginning to feel ex-
> hausted. Stanislav has lost weight and has circles
> under his eyes. Leonard's eyes look red and anx-

Soviet cosmonauts: (left to right, seated) Nikolaev, Belyaev, Tereshkova, Bykovskii, and Popovich; (standing) Volynov, Khrunov, Beregovoi, Shatalov, Eliseev, and Leonov—photographed January, 1969.

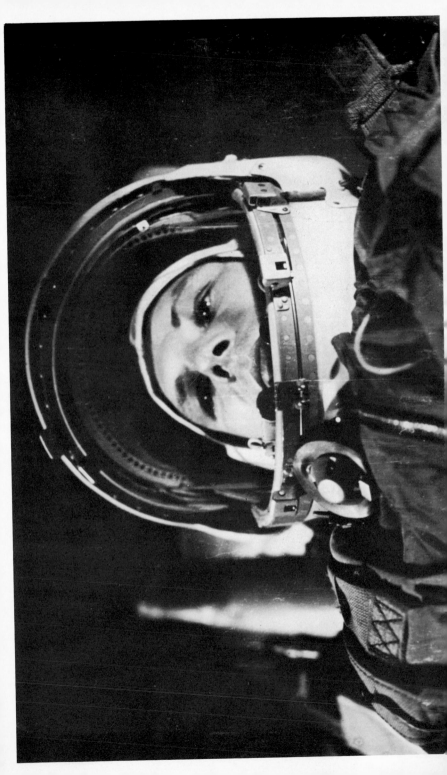

Rocket carrier of the Vostok-1, which was manned by Gagarin. *Tass from Sovfoto*

Yuri Gagarin   *Tass from Sovfoto*   Vladimir Lebedev

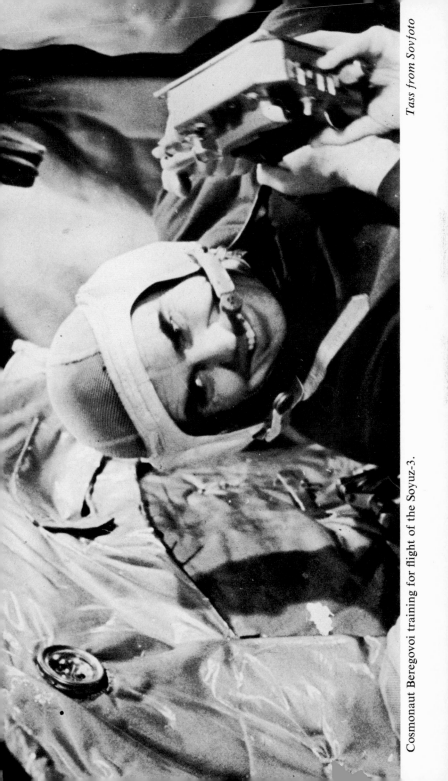

Cosmonaut Beregovoi training for flight of the Soyuz-3.

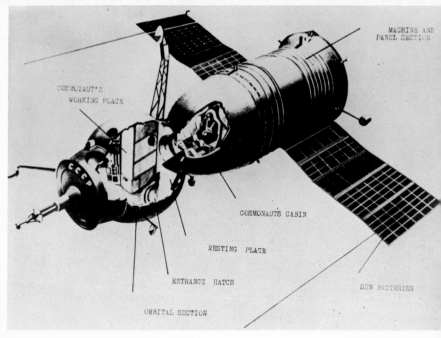

A drawing of the spacecraft Soyuz-3.

Tass from Sovfoto

Beregovoi as shown on television
during the Soyuz-2 flight.

Novosti from Sovfoto

Beregovoi getting ready
for the flight of Soyuz-3.

Novosti from Sovfoto

Yuri Gagarin at a press conference.   *Tass from Sovfoto*

ious. The general tone of the conversation is not always pleasant. There have been flare-ups, very close to fights, over nothing.

[A week later he wrote:] Watch, dinner, medical tests, sleep. Time has become foreshortened. . . . One day is no different from the next. Nervous exhaustion is creeping up on us. We have become more irritable, and it's harder to work. The desire to open the door and see something new is more frequent. Just anything new. Sometimes you want to see a bright color, a red poster, or the blue sky so badly it hurts. Boredom.

The relationship between two doctors, Dr. S. P. Kukishev (44 years old) and Dr. E. I. Gavrikov (25 years old) who spent 45 days in isolation together is vividly described in these excerpts from their diaries:

16th day—GAVRIKOV: My appetite is down noticeably. Since yesterday I've had practically no sleep. It's easier on Petrovich [Kukishev]. Yesterday he was so courteous it was really something. What a guy! The change in rhythm must be easier on him. . . . The experiment is one-third over, and a small conclusion can be drawn. The worst days were the first five before we got used to each other, before we got used to the idea that this was it for 45 days.

I feel like writing and I think the diary will be very satisfying. The conversation is pretty limited. . . . When a man has to work at night, he sleeps during the day, and pays no attention to his metabolic rhythm. He gets up at night all rested, has his dinner, watches television, goes to work. In the morning his metabolic rhythm puts him to sleep. But when you change suddenly to a new regime you notice things about your physiology that you never noticed before. Amazing, frightening things. I feel especially like sleeping between three and seven in the afternoon. . . .

19th day—KUKISHEV: The unattractive sides of my partner's behavior hardly bother me at all. That's all pretty much in the past. Things are much calmer than during the first days of the experiment. We

don't have much in common. There's work, reading, the diaries, and silence. . . .

20th day—GAVRIKOV: Things here in the chamber
are fine, thank God. We don't talk much, less than
we ought, actually, but that's probably why we're
on good terms. Today I wanted so much to go for a
walk.

21st day—GAVRIKOV: I'm amazed at Kukishev's
control. He never cracks; I'm not quite so solid. It
seems to me that we've adjusted. We're sleeping
about the same. During the day, we're cheerful,
hard-working. But nights are something else, the
nervous system doesn't want to change.

24th day—GAVRIKOV: We have an interesting relationship. I still don't understand it. For a while I
didn't care for him, especially at first, now he
seems quite nice sometimes. I could stay with him
again. . . .

24th day—KUKISHEV: On the first or sixth day he
had me so worn out with his moans and groans,
his yawns, his ostentatiously phlegmatic personality, his negative judgments, that it was hard for me
not to give myself away in word, tone, gesture, or
behavior. My diary has been my salvation. Without this channel for pouring out my experiences of
the day and of the moment, one wrong word could
have fatal consequences.

25th day—GAVRIKOV: Today I suddenly wanted
so much to walk the streets, see some trees, half
the summer is gone. . . . S. P. says that he feels
fine, but he's yawning too. He's just as bored as I
am. What's his game? I don't get him. We talk very
little. We don't get along together but we've worked
things out. A life like this at home would have
had me quarreling long since! I never noticed
this about myself but S. P. thinks it's so. . . . I
don't want any quarreling on board our ark. I'm
so sick of this room, its dull green walls, the sealed
doors, the benches, the electrical equipment. . . .
I had an urge to smoke and I told S. P. Self-
indulgence, he says. I don't understand him, but
I could sit it out with him again. Probably because
we'd "rather bear those ills we have than fly to
others that we know not of." It's perfectly possible

to work and live with him. The psychic damage he does is normal. . . . Bombard was right when he wrote that his worst mistake was counting the days. There are maybe three hours a day that hardly seem to move at all. They're the hours when you're depressed or thinking about the family or simply not feeling like doing anything. But in general the days are interesting, they fly past and are forgotten. I can't remember the day before yesterday for example. This week went especially fast. I'd stay here alone without any hesitation, now that I know what it is like.

29th day—KUKISHEV: Everything is changing—mood, perceptions, feelings, our relationship, ability to work, and if you don't write it down right away you forget (sometimes we can't even remember what we had for dinner last) and then you don't believe it was really like that.

30th day—GAVRIKOV: Well, a month of our stay in isolation has passed. What can I say in honor of the occasion? It's a perfectly reasonable length of time and it's been pretty easy for me. The hardest part was probably the first three or four days and the hours from noon to six. But now life has taken on an ordinary rhythm. . . . I still don't understand our relations, but today I thought that we're rather like two people after a reconciliation. As a rule we don't fight. We make no unnecessary conversation. We have a different set of interests and then there's the difference in age. But without a doubt I could sit out another month. I'm sure of that. We know how to make concessions to one another so we can have a normal life and are able to work together fruitfully. We haven't had a single conflict. . . . Today I thought how nice it would be to have just a little bouquet of flowers on the table.

32nd day—GAVRIKOV: Kukishev is right, I've noticed it too. Loss of memory is a strange thing—yesterday I couldn't remember dinner from the night before. It happens constantly. The days pass right through the memory. I'm reading Kukishev more slowly and attentively now. Although our circumstances are different I find much in common in our feelings. We have the same forgetfulness.

The days have become somehow abstract. Food doesn't occupy me much. Books seem to be the best weapons against boredom and apathy. Dear, dear books . . . Today I tried to remember the furniture at home and I couldn't. . . . We are in full agreement about time. Time flies away into nothing, I can't remember what happened, it simply disappears.

36th day—GAVRIKOV: Probably the best thing is how fabulously fast time flies. I'm not talking about the low hours, there aren't too many of them. No matter what I'm doing, reading, simply sitting, doing exercises, time always goes fast. It keeps me in a good mood.

We can see from the excerpts that relations between group members may be diverse, but they usually fall into two general types: business relations binding together people carrying out a specific social goal, and personal relations, joining people on a basis of sympathy or antipathy, attraction or repulsion.

It has been proved that groups bound together only by a common goal (nominal groups) are less stable than groups bound together both by a common goal and by mutual choice, sympathy, and friendship (cohesive groups). Most stable are the so-called homogeneous groups bound together on a basis of common interests and psychic-physiological compatibility. Such groups are highly viable, and can soften or cancel out individual conflicts of tastes and habits.

Group psychology has become the subject of much important research and principles applicable to the assignment of space-flight teams have already been developed. It has become clear that these teams should not only train together but spend their leisure time together. They should get to know each well, because then psychologists and doctors can evaluate the psychic compatibility of the team and "knock it together" by taking out anyone who does not belong in a particular group.

CHAPTER FIVE

Emotions in Space

To be a cosmonaut one need not be a superman. Cosmonauts may have to have great courage, strength,
and fortitude, but nothing human is alien to them.
They have the same emotions of joy, sorrow, worry,
and ecstasy as anyone else. Sometimes our emotions
can mobilize our spiritual powers and enable us to
accomplish the seemingly impossible; at other times
they have the opposite effect. They attack the will
and psyche, rendering a man indecisive and helpless.
The orbital flights and innumerable experiments on
Earth have shown that cosmonauts like pilots are under extreme nervous tension and must have great
willpower and self-control. Therefore, in training cosmonauts much serious attention has been devoted to
the development of willpower.

In the face of danger

Space flights produce amazing scientific discoveries,
introduce completely new and unexpected phenomena, and are naturally very thrilling and satisfying.
But they are dangerous. Because they are experimental in character, no one can completely guarantee
their success.

An English director of an astronomical observatory
said of the space flights: "The risk is so great that it
requires an absolutely new and unprecedented level
of courage. The Russians and Americans have attained that level of courage but we must recognize
the fact that while the risk of an orbital flight is great,
the risk involved in a Moon landing and return to
Earth is simply not worth it." As it approaches the
Moon, the spacecraft "will be moving at a speed of

over 6000 miles per hour. The firing of the retro-rockets—a moment which must be chosen with split-second accuracy—will slow the spacecraft so that it goes into a lunar orbit 60 to 100 miles away from the surface of the Moon." Returning to Earth, "if the spacecraft reenters the atmosphere at the wrong attitude, it will either burn up, or break out of the atmosphere and be forever lost in space."

Nikolaev described his feelings on returning to Earth in this way: "It's a very interesting sensation when the craft begins to burn on reentry. Flames rage and crackle outside the window. You think you must be losing the heat-protective coating on the craft. But I knew better than that. I said to myself, 'Take it easy, let it burn, the descent is going according to plan.' "

Here we have, of course, one of those situations requiring great self-control on the part of the cosmonaut, willpower to put down his natural anxiety, and ability to see things in proper perspective. If a man cannot control his fears, he can fall apart in panic and fail to carry out his responsibilities. Lack of emotional and psychological preparation can leave a man unable to bear nervous-emotional strain and the quality of his work will be severely affected.

When electronic equipment was first used during the Second World War and fliers were required to carry out several operations at once, they began to make mistakes under the strain; they forgot important factors, made inaccurate calculations, lost all ability to evaluate the situation coolly.

An operation such as refueling in midair requires great nerve power. The pilot must maneuver absolutely accurately or else there will be a collision. It is not surprising that in such a situation certain physiological changes occur. The pulse rate goes up to 145 to 160 beats a minute, in beginners sometimes even up to 180, or 2 to 2½ times as high as the normal rate. Respiration rate goes up to 30 to 50 a minute, or 2½ to 3 times as high as normal.

The experience of the American astronauts executing a rendezvous in orbit has shown that this is a much more complicated maneuver than refueling in midair. Using the manual controls the cosmonaut must bring the craft to the rendezvous, slowing down steadily in order to avoid collision. Because the rules of aerodynamics are inapplicable in space, the shortest route to the rendezvous will often be a curved instead of a straight line, requiring a different set of coordinates.

The emotional strain of not having enough time is intense. Army pilot Shtuchkin has described a test flight:

> On approaching the airport a red light went on in the cockpit signaling Lugovoi that he was running out of fuel. It was not really serious; he had time to fly a few more minutes and make an easy landing. But the sight of that signal precluded cool and rational behavior. Going into the landing he forgot to let down the landing gear. The flight commander told him to circle again. The pilot, not taking in the order, continued trying to land. But he had to circle again anyway because he'd already bypassed the airfield.
>
> At an altitude of about 300 feet he made a 180° turn to the right, trying to land opposite the starting point, but seeing that he was still to the left of the landing strip, he tried to angle in.
>
> I was at the airfield that day, and watched it all in disbelief, then with increasing alarm. What's happened to him, I thought. It was as if it was his first time up in a plane, he handled himself so badly.

The pilot neither obeyed the commander's orders nor answered his questions. The landing gear was still up, the plane was in an unnatural bank, and the situation looked hopeless. It was only the composure, persistence, and firmness of the flight commander that saved the pilot's life.

Imagine then the emotional burden of the cosmonaut in an emergency, when for example the automatic control breaks down and he must land the spacecraft manually. The slightest error in firing the retro-rockets will send the spacecraft into another orbit from which it will be impossible to return to Earth. Even when the direction is correct it is always possible that the spacecraft will come down in the wrong spot—in the mountains, forests, ocean, or desert.

As we have said, the automatic control broke down on the Voskhod-2 landing. Captain Belyaev took over the manual controls and fired the retro-rockets at the proper time. He was composed and confident; as an experienced pilot he had had to act in unexpected and difficult situations before and the experience paid off.

One time as a squadron leader Belyaev had to lead a group of planes flying from an island to the mainland. While over water his motor started to give out and the fighter plane began to drop. Belyaev advanced the throttle, but the engine did not respond; obviously there was not enough fuel. The instrument panel showed fuel in the tanks but for some reason the fuel wasn't getting to the engines. He tried the manual fuel pump and the engines responded, the plane stopped dropping. Holding on to the controls with his left hand, Belyaev worked the fuel pump with his right. From the ground the rocking movement of the plane looked very strange but it is impossible to keep a plane on an even keel when one hand is engaged in furious movement, forward and back. After a time his hand went numb, all but refusing to work, but summoning all his strength, Belyaev went on working the fuel pump. By the time he finally landed and got out of the cockpit, his hand was hanging limp and he could no longer raise it.

Another incident involved bad weather. Having completed his mission, Belyaev was on his way back to the airfield when he saw clouds and fog building up. Landing was going to be dangerous and tricky. Orders from the ground were to get down fast.

As Belyaev tells it, there was no time for deliberation. He stepped on the gas and began to bank the plane for a landing. As he did so he pictured the airfield, the previous landings he had made, and made his calculations. The picture in his mind was accurate and precise. Cold shivers ran down his back, though a minute before it had seemed hot in the cabin. It was now time for the dive through the clouds. He looked at the second hand. He was in his last turn. He pushed the stick forward. The plane began to lose altitude. Through the dense shroud he could see the red lights of the landing field coming closer and closer. Then the long-awaited thump of the wheels on the ground. The nightmare was over.

The Americans are going to be operating within strict time limits when they attempt a Moon landing in the Apollo project. They plan to make the landing on manual controls. The astronauts will pick the spot, orient the craft vertically to the surface of the Moon, gradually cutting the speed of the engines, then cutting them off completely for a soft landing. And all this, by their calculations, should take only 75 seconds.

Self-control is particularly important in emergency situations requiring lightning-quick decisions. Here is an episode from a book called *Tested in the Skies* by M. L. Gallai, a test pilot and Hero of the Soviet Union. When he was testing out the Lavochkin-5 his engines failed.

To cap it all, a long tongue of fire from the engines licking at the cockpit window. Puffs of thin blue smoke coming up from the pedals. Of all things, a fire in midair! One of the worst things that can happen to your little island of wood and metal dangling between Earth and sky, carrying 25 gallons of gasoline.

It was a regular aviation circus, displaying itself in all its beauty! As always when I'm in a tight situation, I shuddered and went onto a strange double standard of time. Each second has the magic power to expand to however much time you need to do what you have to do. Time seems to stop.

But no, that's not it. It's that there are no empty
voids, no dragging pauses, no urge to rush time.
On the contrary, time rushes you. It doesn't stop,
it flies even faster than usual. If only you could
always be so adroit, so deft, so efficient!

Working almost automatically—it takes more time
just to tell about it—I decelerated, closed the fuel
lines, set the propellers at minimum revolutions,
and made a sharp turn toward the airfield.

And so with the plane possibly about to explode in
midair, he made a successful landing and saved the
test plane. There are endless examples of similar courage that could be cited. But there have also been
cases—happily quite rare—in which the pilot panicked
and did things that led to catastrophe. Once a plane
burned up, killing two men while the pilot parachuted
out in time. During the investigation the pilot asserted
that before jumping he had given the signal that he
was ditching the plane and had waited several minutes, receiving no answer. In fact it was subsequently
brought out that the interval between the ditching
order and the jump had been only a matter of seconds. The members of the crew could not have had
enough time to jump and save themselves. The tre-
mendous nervous tension was too much for the pilot.
He lost all sense of time and the others lost their lives.

Alarm and fear are not the predominant emotions
of pilots and cosmonauts. Their emotions before and
during a flight are complex and diverse—there is the
natural urge to know the unknown, a sense of duty
and responsibility toward one's mission, excitement,
anxiety—dynamic emotions, shifting and coming together in contradictory combinations.

Gagarin, the first man to orbit the Earth, experienced great joy at being the one to make the flight.
Here is his statement just before blast-off:

Dear friends, family, fellow countrymen, people of
all countries and continents everywhere! In the
next few minutes this great spacecraft is going to

carry me far out into space. What can I tell you in these last minutes before blast-off? I see my whole life as one wonderful preparation for this moment. Everything I've ever been or done has been done for this moment. Can you understand, imagine my feelings when I was picked to make this flight? Was it joy? No, not just joy. Pride? No, not just pride. It was great happiness. To be the first in space, to step into single-handed combat with nature, what more can you ask?

But afterward I thought about the colossal responsibility. The first to accomplish what generations had dreamed of, the first one to lead the way to space. Just name a greater, more complex task than the one that has befallen me. And the responsibility is not to a few dozen people but to the whole collective. A responsibility to the whole of the Soviet people, present and future. And when I accept this flight it is because I am a Communist and have behind me the unprecedented heroism of my fellow countrymen, the Soviet people. I am gathering my forces to do the best job I can. I will do everything in my power to accomplish the task set by the Communist party and the Soviet people.

Am I happy as I start out on this space flight? Of course I'm happy. Throughout history the greatest happiness has always been in participating in great discoveries.

I want to dedicate this first space flight to the peoples under communism, our Soviet people, and one day I am sure, all the peoples of the Earth.

Now there are only minutes until blast-off. Dear friends, as we say when we start off on any long trip, til we meet again. How I'd like to hug you all, friend and stranger, near and far! See you soon!

Positive emotions are helpful, activating. The other emotions depress and demobilize, rendering a man helpless and weak in the face of approaching danger. Would it be somehow possible to control those negative emotions, if not eliminate them altogether?

In a research institute in Atlanta, Georgia, a group

of scientists are working on telesthetic communication
with the brain by means of a small instrument applied
directly to the scalp. It transmits messages such as
"Sleep," "Stay awake," and "Eat" electronically to the
brain. For the moment the experiments are being
made on monkeys, but many officials in American
aeronautical research already consider telethesia the
"ideal means for controlling the behavior of astronauts." They believe that with transmissions from
Earth "the astronauts can be made to sleep, eat, forget their solitude, and be put most on guard in moments of danger." Thus we can not only control emotional behavior but render men generally unemotional.
But just for a moment imagine men without their
emotions: we see soulless robots, lacking all feeling of
friendship, compassion, love, hate, joy. Without emotions human existence would be unthinkable.

The power of emotion

"Things exist outside us. Our perceptions and ideas
are images of those things," Lenin wrote in one of his
philosophical works. Like other psychic processes,
emotions are aroused by a reaction of the nervous
system to existing phenomena. If perceptions and
ideas reflect the objective world, emotions reflect the
subjective phenomena involved in the satisfaction of
man's various needs.

In the behavior of every living creature two stages
can be observed: the stage of formulation of need
and inclination, and the stage of satisfaction. Man's
needs and inclinations can be divided into biological
needs inherited from our ancestors and social needs
arising in the historic process of human development.

A biological need is created by the interaction between the organism and its environment. A change in
the water-salt balance in the blood sends an impulse
to certain structures in the brain and a man begins to
feel thirst. The temperature drops and a man feels

cold. The feelings of thirst, hunger, cold, and pain reflect changes taking place in the organism and its environment.

A social need is the urge for human contact, work, knowledge, or art. Like a biological need, it is accompanied by an emotion that prompts man to do something to satisfy his need.

Emotions are the spontaneous reaction of an individual to his environment. If two men see a dish of appetizing, good-smelling food, they both receive an identical image of a real object in the outside world. But the image will arouse a positive, pleasant emotion in the hungry man, but only indifference or mild repugnance in the full man.

A Communist society is being built in the U.S.S.R. with the labor of the whole Soviet people. A new electric-power station, new homes, a successful feat in space, a good wheat harvest, important scientific discoveries are all causes for joy to us and our friends, but not to those who hate socialism.

Emotions prompt an individual to take actions which affect the outside world. Like acts of will, emotions have an *active* character. Man not only knows the world, he acts upon it, altering it in accord with his needs and goals. Stressing the active character of knowledge and emotion, Engels once observed that "will can be determined either by passion or reflection." By taking care of his needs, man experiences satisfaction and pleasure. "But as long as the need is unsatisfied," wrote Marx, "man is not satisfied, either in his need or with himself."

Innumerable experiments on animals have proved that irritating certain nerve cells in the brain causes pleasant or unpleasant sensations. In one experiment electrodes were attached to various brain spheres in rats, and the animals were able to turn on the current themselves by means of special levers. It developed that with one arrangement of electrodes the rat would work the lever up to eight times an hour, and with another arrangement, it would press the lever once and never go near it again. The scientists surmised that in the first case the electrodes were connected to a "pleasure center," in the second case, a "pain center."

In recent years a method of trepanation has been developed for placing electrodes deep inside the human brain. Subjects remain conscious and report their sensations in detail as various spheres of the brain are stimulated. Stimulation of certain spheres causes satisfaction, high spirits, joy, with the subject frequently asking that the experiment be continued. Stimulation of other spheres causes anxiety, alarm, depression, fear, and terror. Both negative and positive emotions assist man in his accommodation to the constantly changing conditions of the world around him.

The "analytical reflex," as Pavlov called it, is indispensable in a constantly changing situation. We observe a new object, smell it, listen to its sounds. "The strength of our desire to make direct contact with an interesting object," wrote Pavlov, "is evident in all the ropes, barriers, and do-not-touch signs that are necessary in museums to protect the displays from a cultivated public."

"With dogs," Pavlov wrote, "the connections are always practical; an object is edible or inedible, dangerous or safe." In monkeys, "the instinct goes beyond hunger and self-defense to something as independent as disinterested curiosity." Studying a chimpanzee named Rosa, Pavlov came to the conclusion that "she prefers mental exercise to the satisfaction of her stomach. Give her something to do and something to eat and she'll push the food away. So one can then say that if she is more interested in solving problems, it must be on the basis of curiosity."

In the man the thirst for knowledge is bound up with the emotions and passions. "Without 'human emotion' human search for truth could never have been and never could be," Lenin wrote.

Imagine the emotions of a man like Giordano Bruno, the Italian philosopher burned at the stake during the Inquisition in the name of truth. Or the Russian revolutionary and inventor Nikolai Kibalchich, who though condemned and imprisoned by the tsar, worked up to the day of his death inventing the idea of a jet-propelled aircraft. Or Tsiolkovskii who, without any special education, deprived of research facilities, held in contempt by his contemporaries, still went on to lay the foundation for rocket building and interplanetary flight.

Passion and enthusiasm are required of cosmonauts in training. Vladimir Komarov had fulfilled a childhood dream by becoming a pilot. Then, scarcely daring to hope, he put in his application to become a cosmonaut. Shortly after he was accepted, he had to be hospitalized and undergo an operation, the aftereffects of which left grave doubts about his future participation in space flights. It required great persistence on his part to convince the doctors he could go back into service. His superior officer wrote: "He badgered the army doctors, he went to the commanding officers. He proved himself over and over again. We made calls. You could see Vladimir's passionate dedication breaking them down. His comrades were all for him. They kept asking, arguing, insisting that he be included in the group. It was finally decided that he be put back into training and watched."

Within five months Komarov had caught up with his comrades and become a cosmonaut in good standing. They named him backup man for the Vostok-3 and Vostok-4 flights, but again he was unfortunate. During his tests in the centrifuge heart trouble was discovered. They took him out of training, and again the question of his fitness was raised. But his heart trouble proved temporary, and the dream to which he had clung so steadfastly came true. Komarov was made captain of Voskhod-1, the first spacecraft to carry three men into orbit.

On April 24, 1967, Komarov gave his life on Soyuz-1 for the future conquest of space.

Interacting with an environment that is potentially dangerous, a man must be able to appraise new phenomena incredibly fast and act accordingly. But sometimes the factors are so many and diverse that they cannot be analyzed quickly, if at all. Encountering a new phenomenon, a man may not have enough time or experience or knowledge to deal with it. He will then have to be saved by the emotional instinct which reacts to a series of objects and phenomena and can answer the basic question: Is this new thing good or dangerous?

The speed of analysis and reaction is especially important when the organism has already begun to feel the effect of the unexpected factor. A man reacts immediately to a harmful factor like a snakebite or a burn because he experiences pain. Tasting an unfamiliar food a man will find it bitter, sweet, tasty, unappetizing and either eat it or push it away.

But there are harmful phenomena that act so quickly that the organism has no time to protect itself; a man is injured or dies. Thus it becomes imperative that new phenomena be evaluated at a distance. The information gathered by the long-distance senses—optic, aural, chemical—can arouse either a positive or negative emotion. Looking into an abyss a man feels an instinctive fear although he may never in his life have fallen from a great height. This is an innate reaction developed over the course of evolution, dating from the time man's ancestors were falling from cliffs or trees and killing or mutilating themselves.

Innate emotional reactions are present in the decision whether something is edible. When a hungry man comes upon something unfamiliar, appearance and smell can arouse either appetite or revulsion. Thus the smell of strawberries usually causes a pleasant sensation, spoiled meat—revulsion.

Though the sensations aroused by an encounter with new phenomena may turn out to be erroneous, they play an important role. Emotions represent the most common reaction to useful or harmful factors developed throughout evolution. Thanks to these instinctive emotions man can react instantaneously and behave accordingly.

Pavlov correctly observed that nature would not allow experience acquired by creatures during the course of a lifetime to be lost; certain conditioned reflexes are passed on to succeeding generations. But he also repeatedly stressed that instinctual reactions in human beings appear in their purest form only during a very short period of time after birth. After that, in specific response to the specific environment, conditioned reflexes develop that affect the emotions.

But it is not merely concrete events and phenomena that arouse the emotions. Secondary signals, or words, can be just as powerful stimuli. Pavlov characterizes the secondary signal system as a "new principle of nervous activity—words are an abstraction and generalization of innumerable other signals, and in turn an analysis and systematization of those generalized signals—a principle providing unlimited orientation in the environment."

Verbal stimuli are to be distinguished from direct stimuli in their universality—verbal stimuli can replace direct stimuli and elicit the same response from the organism. Even verbal stimuli that do not correspond to objective reality can elicit a specific emotional response. Take the case of the cosmonaut candidate who flunked the tests in the centrifuge because of his heightened emotional state. The cosmonaut was taped with electrodes and put into the cabin. Without turning on the centrifuge, the tester running the experiment began calling out acceleration stress through the microphone: 1, 2, 3, 4 G's, etc. The centrifuge was motionless but the cosmonaut's pulse and respiration rate rose sharply, reaching 190 and 50 respectively, and the electroencephalograph also registered changes typical of high acceleration stress.

Each man is a "fusion" of innate and acquired emotions, and the character of that fusion depends on his nervous system and environment in the broad sense of the word. Thus men encountering absolutely identical phenomena will react differently; what moves one will not touch another.

The doctors remain behind

No matter how hard a man tries to hide his feelings, his psychic activity will somehow find an outward expression. "When a baby laughs at the sight of a toy, when Garibaldi smiles when he is run out of his country, when a girl trembles in first love, when Newton conceives universal laws and puts them down on paper, the final fact is always muscular movement," I. M. Sechenov wrote nearly 100 years ago.

Human emotions can be judged from involuntary expressions of the face, bodily movements, speech intonation. Certain emotional states (anger, joy, sorrow, fear, amazement) correspond exactly to certain facial expressions, revealing what mood a man is in, what feelings possess him.

Charles Darwin established that expressive physical movements were developed in the process of evolution and once were of vital importance. Teeth gnashing, for example, flared nostrils, fists clenched in anger, all at one time necessary to our animal ancestors, were strengthened in the process of natural selection and passed along from generation to generation. One can find any number of examples in Darwin of similar emotional expressions in men and animals.

In the process of historic development many of man's adaptive reactions, including these primitive physical expressions, have ceased to be as necessary as they once were, but they have nonetheless persisted in innate and involuntary mechanisms in the nervous system. But in man even the simplest emotions are not as stereotyped as in an animal. They are more complex and many-hued.

The emotional state of the cosmonauts in flight could be judged, apart from everything else, from the expressions on their faces. Who can forget Bykovskii's gay smiling face on television when he demonstrated various objects swimming around in weightlessness.

The cosmonauts' speech was subjected to careful analysis by psychologists and doctors for intonation and emotional coloration. The tone in which a cosmonaut said he was feeling fine was more important to the psychologist than the sense of the words.

Unexpected, unplanned questions and jokes made by cosmonauts to their comrades in the tracking stations testify to their good spirits and emotional equilibrium. Nikolaev's interest in the final soccer match in Kubok and Popovich's congratulations to the Miners' soccer team was as good a testimony to their mood and state of mind as their pulse and respiration rates.

One of the signs of intense emotional activity is increased muscular activity. We know that in a state of great anger or fear man exhibits what is for him unusual energy—he can run faster or jump farther.

Pavlov revealed the reason for the link between the emotions and muscular movement. He said in one of his lectures:

> If we turn back to our distant forefathers we see that everything then depended on the muscles. . . . One cannot imagine a beast lying in anger for hours without muscular expression of that anger. Our forebears were in no way different from wild beasts and their every emotion put their muscles to work. When a lion is angry, for example, the emotion pours out in the form of a fight; when a rabbit is scared, there is another sort of activity—running. With our zoological ancestors there was the same sort of direct outpouring into some kind of muscular, skeletal activity—they ran from danger, threw themselves on an enemy, defended the life of a child, etc.

Studies of dozens of men parachuting for sport have shown that jumping not only teaches professional skills like separation from the aircraft, use of the chute, and landing; it also develops qualities of purposefulness, composure, self-control, decisiveness, daring. This is why parachute jumping has occupied such an important place in the training of cosmonauts.

The emotions change during the course of the jumps and the dynamics of that process are particularly apparent during the first stage of cosmonaut training. Dynamometric readings of hand strength taken from Titov, Nikolaev, Popovich, and others on the first day of the jumps rose from 4 to 18 pounds, indicating an emotional reaction to the experiment. Two other cosmonauts who had intended to participate in the jumps announced just before starting time that they would not jump, and their dynamometric readings dropped sharply.

Muscular movement is subordinate to the will of man, but this is not the case with muscle tone or tension when a man is in an emotional state. Nerve impulses coming from the central nervous system and the secretion of adrenalin significantly increase muscle tone. Increased muscle tone is sometimes accompanied by tremors which are explained by the imbalance in tension between the separate muscle groups. Muscular activity in turn requires an increased circulation of oxygen and the products of oxidation.

Since ancient times men have associated their emotions with the heart. It is no accident that we speak of the heart "knocking with fear," "jumping with joy," or "stopping."

The doctors of antiquity evaluated a patient's emotional state by the rate and quality of the heartbeat. The great Arab physician, philosopher, and mathematician known in Europe as Avicenna was once called to a young prince who was "wasting away," unable to eat or sleep. Avicenna guessed that the young man was in love and advised that he marry his beloved, after which the invalid quickly recovered his health.

In 1020, in his *Canon of Medical Science*, Avicenna wrote:

> Love is an illness like illusion, like melancholia. To determine the love object is one method of cure. The method is this: Call out names repeatedly while taking the pulse. When the pulse rate changes sharply and becomes erratic, check that name again and again and you will know the name of the beloved. In the same way you can call out street names, houses, trades, occupations, genealogies, and towns in combination with the name of the beloved, still taking the pulse; as it changes with the repetition of one or another of these names, you will gather all the information about the beloved, her clothes, her activities, and her identity. We used this method and were able to establish the identity of the beloved. If you can find no other cure than bringing the two together according to faith and law, then do it.

Though they stayed behind on earth, doctors were able to follow the state of health and emotional reactions of the cosmonauts on the first space flights by telemeters. Small silver electrodes were taped to the body and head to measure the electrical activity of the heart and brain. These electrical impulses multiplied thousands of times by telemeter on board the spacecraft were transmitted to Earth and decoded. Thus doctors on Earth could watch the pulse and respiration rates, the electrocardiograms and electroencephalograms.

On the active part of the flight Gagarin's pulse rate went up to 157 a minute. When that rate was compared to his pulse rate during acceleration stress tests in the centrifuge, it was deemed fully normal.

On an actual flight Leonov's heartbeat rate went higher than it had in training. Leonov seems not to have been able to adjust to weightlessness immediately and was under some strain. Later, after he was in orbit, his pulse returned to practically what it had been during training. Then during his space walk and return to the craft his heartbeat rose again. This seems to have been primarily a result of the blindingly bright Sun. "The first thing that struck you was that powerful flood of light," recalls Leonov. "It was like looking straight into an electric welder."

The great physical effort involved in getting back through the spacecraft hatch also played a role. "I took off the movie camera which had recorded my walk in space and tried to get through the hatch. It turned out not to be so easy. Your movements are rather limited in a space suit and the camera was a problem: every time I started toward the hatch it kept getting in my way. It was quite a physical effort and my space walk was a bit longer than planned."

Leonov, our first man to walk in space, suffered no greater emotional tension than the other cosmonauts on that flight. That this is so is thanks to the training program which laid such special emphasis on parachute jumping.

On the threshold

When you look down from a rooftop unguarded by railings you become dizzy and afraid. The physiological mechanism involved is this: The perception of height sets off a special danger signal to the cortex of the brain where the point of excitation, by the law of induction, spreads to other sections of the brain. When the process of inhibition takes hold of the motor-nerve center all motor activity is inhibited. A similar phenomenon is known to schoolboys and students who know their material perfectly but in their extreme nervousness forget and are unable to answer the questions on the exam. The same thing can happen to a man who forgets what he wanted to say to an audience the minute he gets on the platform. He tries to speak, then just waves his hand and steps down. In these cases it is not just the motor-nerve center that is affected but all those sections of the brain containing the schoolwork or the prepared speech.

The biological sense of a man's physical reaction to heights ensures minimal activity on the part of the organism at a time when the slightest careless motion could lead to a fall.

Tsiolkovskii imagined a walk in space in his science-fiction story "Beyond Earth": "When we opened the door and I saw myself standing on the threshold of space I was terrified. I made a convulsive movement that shoved me out of the rocket. I was already used to hanging in midair inside the cabin, but when I saw the abyss beneath me, nothing around me anywhere, I really felt awful. I pulled myself together only when the line had played out tight and I was a kilometer from the rocket." Thus the founder of space science foresaw that the walk in space would be accompanied by a struggle with agoraphobia—a struggle innate and emotional as well as intellectual.

Parachute instructors and psychologists observing a group of parachute trainees reported that they deviated from their normal behavior pattern during training. The deviations grew increasingly marked as the day of the jump approached. The men became increasingly concerned about the jump and how it would come out. They worried that the chute might not work, and that there were no safeguards as there are in other sports. On the last day before the jump many cosmonauts were in a state of acute anxiety. Pulse rates, respiration rates, blood pressures were up. Some lost their appetite. One had a nightmare in which his parachute did not open.

We know that while man can control his attention and thought and other psychic processes, not all psychic functions are equally subject to conscious control. The emotional reaction to heights is far from always within the control of the parachutist. He can suppress the outward manifestations of his anxiety and fear only up to a point.

"Don't believe anyone who tells you he was never afraid. It's not true," writes A. Yarov, a master jumper. "Everyone has an hour, a minute, a second of fear. Once in awhile someone will give in to fear and lose control completely. Others can fight it. You've got that ring in your hand, the straps holding you together. You have the support without which existence is unthinkable—it's just that it's over your head instead of under your dangling feet. The chute opens up over your head like a great white flower. An open chute is as much reassurance and safety as ground under your feet."

Jumping for the first time, the parachutist is nervous, worried, restless, unsure of himself. Movements are often hasty, convulsive, to no purpose. Not having finished one thing, he'll take up another. Sometimes he'll check one part of his equipment over and over again. He loses his voice.

This subjectively painful and unpleasant state is rather similar to the state of soldiers before a battle. Professor G. E. Shumkov, who took part in the Russo-Japanese War, made some interesting observations of soldiers on the eve of battle. Going into battle for the first time they were anxious, uncharacteristically nervous. They felt "on pins and needles" or "on the coals." They exhibited a heightened sensitivity to ordinary irritants: their boots pinched more than usual, their footcloths were wrapped wrong. They would dress and undress as if their uniform were the cause of their distress. They became maladroit with cigarette papers and matches. They found it hard to concentrate on anything. There were individual variations in behavior, however: some couldn't sit still, some were self-restrained, some were completely quiet. They were tortured by thirst, some experienced chills and fever.

Shumkov distinguished between this state of anxiety or anxious expectation and the ordinary state of fear. It is an emotional state familiar in various sports and known as "pregame fever."

Those jumping for the first time react variously. Some turn pale, their pupils become distended, and their mouths and throats go dry. They grow rigid, they tremble, they are absolutely indifferent to everything around them. "That which in psychology we call fear, cowardice, or timorousness," wrote Pavlov, "has as its physiological substratum the inhibitory state of the cortex of the brain and it represents the various stages of the passive-active reflex."

Others jumping for the first time become excited. Their movements become chaotic, their attention wanders, and it is difficult for them to concentrate. Sometimes, though rarely, such a reaction can turn into total panic.

The best reaction is the so-called "fighting spirit." Its physiological precondition is a certain equilibrium between the stimulatory and inhibitory processes in the central nervous system. In this case the necessary factors are all combined: heightened physical ability, intensified perceptual and ratiocinative powers, concentration. The cosmonauts in a state of "fighting preparedness" looked excited but not agitated. Their movements were energetic and coordinated. They carried out orders accurately and on time. The relatively high level of emotional stability in all the cosmonauts can be explained, as we have said, by careful medical and psychological selection, as well as by previous flying experience.

Almost everyone standing in the hatch or on the wings of an airplane for the first time finds it hard to look at the ground. They usually say it takes their breath away, or that it's like a blow on the head, or that their heart did flips. Curiously, even experienced parachutists find jumps from a parachute tower harder than jumps from an airplane. Apparently this is because with a tower jump there is still a "ground sense," which disappears at higher altitudes. The distances made possible by the invention of airplanes appear more abstract and less threatening than those known by our forefathers.

With the commands "Get ready, get set, go!" tension reaches its highest point. This is the moment requiring maximum willpower to overcome innate fear. Physiologically the process of overcoming a fear of heights can be thought of as a strong point of excitation in the secondary signal system.

Words are one of the strongest means of influence on the thoughts, feelings, desires, and behavior of man. They provide a stimulus that can have a profound effect on a man even in a situation where he is in conflict with himself. But words can be powerless when fear has brought a man to a state of virtual numbness: he wants to jump, yet he cannot.

Master jumper V. G. Romaniuk, veteran of 3000 jumps, has described working with a doctor who was jumping for the first time:

> When the plane attained the necessary altitude and reached the jumping zone, I told him to get ready . . . the doctor got out on the wing and stood on the very edge. . . .
>
> "Go!" I said. But the doctor appeared not to hear the order. He stood paralyzed by the abyss under his feet and did not move.
>
> "Come back in!" I ordered. But he stayed as before, obviously too afraid to move. His chute will still open, I thought, banking the plane sharply to the left and gunning the engine.
>
> The doctor dropped from the wing like a stone. The chute opened automatically; he didn't pull the ring himself. It was the first time I'd ever seen such a thing. He landed OK, looking pale but satisfied.
>
> "You angry with me?" I asked him later.
>
> "Frankly, I don't remember what happened up there," he admitted.

Andrian Nikolaev has described his experience this way:

> My jumps were all different. The first time I just about disgraced myself. I remember when we got up there and I looked out, my heart just stopped. When I thought about climbing out of the cabin and onto the wing, I had the horrible urge to ask the instructor to stop the experiment. But he was looking at me and smiling. "Just hang on to the air, hang on to it!"
>
> I was in no mood for jokes. What was it that helped? Being used to discipline. If you had to, you had to. I climbed back to the back cabin where the instructor was sitting. He withdrew the safety lock on my parachute and said, "Go!"
>
> "Go" where when your body is frozen? I wanted to but I couldn't. Gathering all my strength I yanked my hands from the cabin and jumped.

After dropping away from the aircraft a man falls freely in space for some time before his chute opens. To the trained jumper free fall is a pleasure. Those jumping for the first time seem not to remember it. They remember what took place before they heard the jump order, but the jump itself, their feelings about it, the wind direction, the position of their body—all that escapes from memory. All that remains is the moment the parachute opens. "I don't remember leaving the plane," writes Bykovskii, "just the chute shooting up over my head."

In the first seconds of the fall a man is in a state of weightlessness which as we know sharply alters the information going from the inner ear to the brain. In addition, the jumper is being buffeted by airstreams and subjected to changes in barometric pressure and air temperature. All these stimuli fall on the "soil" of a previous emotional state in which he had to battle with himself and to overcome by force of will his fear of heights.

Starting with the second or third jump the jumper can remember and recall his acts and feelings during free fall because his organism has already become accustomed to the extraordinary stimuli and the emotional strain is reduced.

Those who do remember their first jump say that the period of free fall seemed endless though it in fact lasted but a few seconds. Here for example is Gagarin's recollection:

> Ever since childhood I haven't liked to wait. Especially when I knew things were going to be difficult or dangerous. Better to meet it head on than shirk it or put it off. That was why I was so glad after the practice jump when my instructor Dmitrii Pavlovich called, "Gagarin! Board the plane!"
>
> I could hardly breathe. It was still my first real parachute jump. I don't remember anymore what altitude we were flying at. All I can see is my instructor waving me out onto the wing. Well, I got myself out of the cabin somehow and onto the wing, holding on with both hands. I was scared to look down at the ground, it was so far, far away. Terrible.
>
> "Hey Yuri, no fooling around!" my instructor called out. "You ready?"
>
> "Ready," I answer.
>
> "So go!" I push off from the side of the airplane the way I've been taught and hurtle into the abyss. I pull the ring and the chute doesn't open. I want to shout, but I can't, the air has taken my breath away. My hand starts automatically groping for the emergency chute. Where is it? Where is it? Then there's a stiff jerk, and silence. I'm rocking back and forth in the sky under the white emergency chute. It opened in time. I'd thought of it too soon. So that was my first lesson: When you're in the air, trust technology. Don't do anything rash.

With the opening of the chute, the jumper's mood changes abruptly, all the negative emotions are over, and there is a feeling of joy. Jumpers jumping for the first time begin calling out to each other and singing. Usually they don't pay much attention to the landing. One jumper recalls: "I was so carried away I didn't get ready to land. When I finally looked down I realized how fast I was falling. I hadn't felt the speed at all before. There were just 10 or 20 yards to go when I pulled up my legs and got in position, all my attention focused on the ground. I felt a hard blow. I landed on my side practically in the center of the airfield, beside myself with joy."

A successful jump brings on a "permissive" emotional reaction—a particular kind of letdown after psychic tension. Inexperienced jumpers are unable to view their own behavior objectively. The majority assert categorically, "It wasn't frightening. I wasn't a bit afraid." Many are ready to make another jump immediately. The ability to evaluate their emotions realistically and think critically only returns several hours later or the next day, when the excitement has passed.

In order to experience what a cosmonaut feels on a parachute jump, one of the authors, V. Lebedev, a doctor by profession, also took to the air. He had studied jumpers and their reactions, and had a pretty good theoretical understanding of the complications that could arise from a faulty parachute, a bad jump or landing. Here is what he wrote in his diary:

The night before the jump I couldn't sleep. I kept waking up, and was wide awake by five o'clock. Although I tried not to think about it my thoughts kept coming back to the details of a bad jump, and to tragedy.

In the morning I went to get a parachute with several others, three of whom had jumped before. When we had our chutes we took a bus to the airfield.

It was a sunny winter morning. Having already donned the chute, I kept asking myself, Can I really overcome my fear and jump out of the plane?

Valentina Tereshkova and I exchanged roles. Usually it was I who took her pulse before a jump. Now she took mine. "Doctor!" she said, "don't worry so much. Your pulse is 110. Your heart will be in your mouth in a minute."

After checking the chutes we took our places in the plane. The plane taxied out to the runway, took off, and quickly gained altitude. I looked out the window and watched the ancient hilly river city and the monastery disappear. I took my own pulse. 130! Across from me was master jumper Valerii Galaida and two comrades jumping for the first time, and they certainly looked different. Valerii was smiling and talking about something with the instructor, N. K. Nikitin. The other two were sitting, their faces pale masks. There was tension and strain in their attitude and in every gesture. Looking at them I thought that I must look no better. Time was going very slowly. The plane seemed to be standing still. All you wanted to do was to get out of the situation as soon as possible.

Nikitin gave the order to get set. I got up, but my legs were like cotton. I forced myself over to the hatch. I was the second one to jump after Galaida. I stood staring at his back, trying not to look down. I heard the order to jump. Galaida gave the hatch door a light shove and was out of the plane, sprawling in air. I don't remember how I got out of the plane. I just felt myself being pulled and turned. I looked up and saw the parachute open over my head. I looked down and saw Galaida's chute. In the silence I could hear the ecstatic cry of one of the other jumpers, "Great!" It really was. The dark blue sky, the bluish snow sparkling in the Sun, the blue bus standing by looking like a toy, the silence after the noise of the engines.

Before the jump I had wanted to take my pulse immediately after the chute opened but I didn't remember until a minute or two had passed. For a while it seemed as if I weren't dropping, just hanging suspended by the chute. Being unable to judge distances I got ready to land way ahead of time by drawing up my knees and sticking my feet out. I stayed in that position for a while, then I grew tired and hung free again. I heard voices calling from the ground, "Feet, feet!" I had just managed to get them together when I felt myself sink into a snowbank. Immediately afterward, like the rest of my comrades, I asked permission to jump again. But the evening after the jump was not so delightful. I went to sleep worrying about the next jump.

Sharpening the will

The skills of handling one's body in space before the chute opens gradually develop on subsequent jumps. The jumper learns to execute complicated turns, spirals, forward and backward somersaults during free fall. Finally he develops the ability to judge time with split-second accuracy.

Just how much a man's emotional state can change as he acquires experience in jumping can be seen in these notes kept on Aleksei Leonov:

1st day: Just after donning the chute, his face turned quite pale. His movements were slow and constrained. His face was uncharacteristically inexpressive. After the jump he perked up a bit, you could still feel the constraint.

2nd day: In much better spirits. If he was constrained the first day, today he was overexcited. His eyes were shining, he was extraordinarily talkative and full of superfluous motions. His speech and facial expressions were animated. After the jump, in a good mood, joked a lot.

3rd day: Well in control of himself. After the jump in a gay mood, joking uninterruptedly.

5th day: Well in control of himself before the jump. Cool and composed. Made two jumps with a 10-second delay on opening the chute. Very little flex in the separation from the aircraft. During free fall movements of the upper and lower extremities uncoordinated. Uncertain and not quite accurate in pancaking.

6th day: A jump with a 15-second delay on opening the chute. Not enough flex in the separation. Position of body in space during free fall unsteady —arms too widely, feet too closely, spaced. Chute opened at 13.8 seconds. During pancaking the chute managed more confidently.

8th day: Made two jumps with a 20-second delay on opening the chute. Mood beforehand serious, concentrated, collected. Good flex in the separation. First part of free fall unsteady. From 12–20 seconds steady in free fall. The chute opened at 20.2 seconds. On the second jump, everything carried out correctly. Handled the chute confidently. After the second jump, mood elated. Obviously pleased with himself.

21st day: Made a jump with a 50-second delay on opening the chute. Before the jump collected, concentrated. Good control of his body in free fall. Opened chute at 50.8 seconds. Despite a rather stiff wind managed the chute correctly and confidently. After the jump, happy, smiling, full of jokes.

On the basis of these observations the following conclusions were drawn about Leonov: During the first two jumps there was considerable emotional tension, but after the second jump he was able to summon his willpower and exercise self-control. The skills of body control in free fall and pancaking the chute were rather quickly mastered. He stood out from the group of cosmonaut trainees for his strong will, rapid mastery of new skills, and ability to adapt to extraordinary circumstances. After 30 jumps he was given the title of jump instructor and by the time of the Voskhod-2 flight he had made 117 jumps of varying complexity.

The lessening of emotional tension is apparent not only in the outward behavior of the cosmonauts but objectively. The first-day pulses taken before takeoff and again on the plane are all up sharply from normal, and dynamometric readings of hand strength are nearly always up. On subsequent jumps these indexes return to normal and the excitement and tension decrease, although they never fully disappear even in experienced jumpers.

But the emotional reaction to danger takes various forms. It does not always galvanize the consciousness. Danger puts some men in a state of actual emotional shock. In others behavior remains basically rational though less effective. A third group maintains complete self-control, displaying resourcefulness and quick-wittedness. These people are often called "crisis lovers." Their reaction to danger is galvanization, the so-called fighting spirit which gets special satisfaction out of overcoming difficulties and fear.

As an example, here are the notes made on Popovich during his training.

> *5th day:* A jump with a 15-second delay on opening the chute. Before the jump tense and absorbed. No flex in the separation from the plane. Unsteady in free fall. Going into a spin he opened the chute at 8 seconds. After landing, upset about imperfect performance, obviously dissatisfied with himself.
>
> *6th day:* A jump with a 20-second delay on opening the chute. Before the jump, calm. Separated from the plane slightly flexed. In first 7 seconds body position unsteady, then the correct position was assumed. Opened chute at 20.2 seconds. Happy and excited afterward. Smiling, he said he now understood his earlier mistakes. Mood cheerful and elated.

Popovich's psychic state thus depended on his performance. Although he was not able to master the skills of free fall immediately, he was able to discover the reasons for his failures, summon his strength, and improve his performance.

But sometimes, when there are repeated failures or physical injuries, subsequent jumps do not lessen tension, rather they increase it. Great willpower is then required to overcome fear and restore one's faith in oneself. Pavel Belyaev demonstrated such willpower. He and Leonov were making a jump with a 30-second delay on chute opening. Everything was going well as they neared the ground. But a strong wind came up suddenly, carrying the men away from the center of the airfield, and they could do nothing to stop it. They both knew it, but tried at least to keep within the limits of the field.

Belyaev pulled the shroud line. He started falling faster, with noticeably less drift. The ground was coming closer and closer, just a few more yards. There was a stiff thud, a sideways rebound, and the chute was dragging him across the grass. His leg was twisted and painful. Broken, he thought, still trying to stop himself. Comrades ran up, unstrapped him, and got him to his feet. After 15 yards both legs gave out. It took several others to get him back.

The pain became unbearable. The impact with the ground had been strong enough to knock the heels off both boots. Belyaev was sent to the hospital for a "spiral fracture of both the tibia and fibula of the left leg with scattered fragments."

For nearly six months he lay in the hospital. For a whole year he had to stay out of training, falling way behind his comrades. But then it was time to start jumping again. The doctors were worried that the broken leg might have made him fearful.

And so there was Belyaev in the air again. It was winter and the airfield was buried in deep snow. The weather was fine. Everything looked favorable for a successful jump.

The group divided into pairs. The first pair to jump was Gagarin and Belyaev. No sooner had they jumped than a stiff wind came up over the ground. It became clear they weren't going to be able to land on the airfield. The two worked their shroud lines, but they were being relentlessly carried toward a railroad bed, a high-voltage power line, and a lumber yard. It didn't take a specialist to know the danger they were in.

On the airfield people were anxiously watching the jumpers. Gagarin landed not far from the railroad track and signaled that he was all right. Belyaev went on over the railroad track, over the high power line, and dropped behind a lumberyard building. A cross-country truck equipped with medical supplies headed for the spot.

Belyaev was standing there calmly, surrounded by lumberyard workers. It turned out that when he realized that the wind was carrying him into the lumberyard he spotted a small building among the log piles and decided to land on the roof. It took accuracy and self-control to make use of his one chance of saving himself from landing on the log piles. There was a second jump, a third, seven test jumps, and he successfully passed them all.

CHAPTER SIX

In a Weightless World

Weightlessness was a new phenomenon. We had to get out into space in order to really understand it, yet we also had to know in advance how it was going to affect man. The fact that living creatures on our planet have always lived under the enormously powerful force of gravity could not be forgotten or underestimated. Gravity determined the size, shape, and physiological functions of animals, and in human beings a specific set of psychic-physiological mechanisms had to be developed to counteract the force of gravity and keep the body in a vertical position. Now this new phenomenon. How would man take it?

The end of the world

On purely theoretical premises, Tsiolkovskii assumed that in space man would suffer from illusions and lose his bearings. He also assumed that even so, man would be able to adjust to his new condition. "The illusions," he wrote, "at least inside the spacecraft, ought to disappear."

Since Tsiolkovskii's time there has been much speculation about the effect of weightlessness on the organism and on psychic activity. Skeptics were convinced that an extended state of weightlessness would be impossible for man to endure, and so the first experiments with rockets in outer space were made with animals. The second stage of experimentation was on men in a state of temporary weightlessness (20 to 30 seconds) in jet airplanes.

Today both in our country and abroad there is a vast amount of scientific literature on the effect of weightlessness on psychic and physiological functions. In their reactions it seems men can be divided into three groups.

In the first group are those who can sustain temporary weightlessness without noticeable difficulty. They are able to go right on working, experiencing only a slight limpness or relaxation as a result of the "loss" of weight. All the Soviet cosmonauts belonged to this group.

Here are the notes made by Gagarin after a flight in a two-seated plane and a period of temporary weightlessness. "Before banking the flight was normal; when it banked I was pinned to my chair; then the chair moved out from under me and my feet came up off the floor. I looked at the instrument panel; it showed 0 G's, weightlessness. A pleasant feeling of lightness. I tried moving my hands and head, I felt light and free. I grabbed at a pencil and the oxygen hose floating in front of me. I could still get my bearings. I could see the sky, the ground, beautiful cumulus clouds."

The second group includes those who experience the sensation of falling, of turning upside down, at the onset of weightlessness, creating a state of anxiety, loss of orientation, inability to perceive correctly. This state, lasting from two to six seconds, changes in a number of cases to a state of euphoria, during which they become playful and joyous and forget what they are supposed to be doing. A leading American psychologist has written, "I have never in my whole life experienced anything so damned pleasant as weightlessness. If I were asked again to choose any form of recreation, I'd undoubtedly choose weightlessness."

Here are excerpts from Lebedev's diary, after a test in the space laboratory, in the "weightlessness pool":

Up to the time of the first "turn" I was sitting strapped to my chair. From the sound of the engines and from the vibration I guessed we were going to "bank." After a few seconds acceleration force threw me back in my chair. Then with the onset of weightlessness I felt I was falling through space. That lasted, I think, one or two seconds. My comrades started floating past me. My parachute slowly came out from under my chair and hung in front of me. Everyone looked strange—one man with his feet in the air, another on his side. They were turning somersaults, getting into odd positions, bumping against the floor, the ceiling, the walls, flying around me. Everything seemed strange and amusing. Being pretty well versed theoretically in the feelings of weightlessness, I expected to take it hard, but it was just the opposite, it was ecstasy. I made the thumbs-up sign to my comrades. Then weightlessness passed and acceleration stress set in again.

When we "banked" again, I was supposed to float free. I put on a protective helmet and lay on the thickly matted floor. Acceleration stress started, driving me into the mat. Immediately after that, weightlessness set in. Before I could collect myself, I felt as if I were flying up, any which way. I was completely disoriented. Then I began to get the picture: I saw the floor and the walls, which seemed to be stretching. It was like looking through the wrong end of binoculars. I looked at the floor and saw it moving under me. I tried to get hold of something. But though things seemed close I just couldn't touch them with my hands. Then, feeling myself at the tail of the plane, I grabbed at something and got my bearings.

It is not only perception of space and surrounding objects that changes. Some men lose "body sense," that is, the conception of the form and size of their body, of the absolute and relative size of various bodily parts, their interaction and the movements of extremities. One of the first pilots to experience weightlessness said, "Within 8 to 10 seconds from the onset of weightlessness I felt as if my head were swelling and expanding in size. After 13 seconds I felt as if my body were spinning slowly in no particular direction.

After 15 seconds I began to lose my bearings in space so I took the plane out of the parabola."

Included in the second group are those who experience a feeling of alienation and helplessness in the state of weightlessness.

> In the first seconds after weightlessness [an experienced pilot admitted], I felt the plane turn over and fly in a transverse position. My head was hanging down. I looked out the window and saw the horizon, and became convinced that I was wrong. Then the illusion disappeared. During the entire period of weightlessness I had an unpleasant, hard-to-describe, and unfamiliar sensation of unnaturalness and helplessness. I felt that something had changed not just in the plane but in myself. Trying to rid myself of this unpleasant feeling, I wanted to try writing in weightlessness and made a grab for my writing things. I was able to do this without special difficulty but the helpless, uncertain feeling continued to torture me.

It must be said for those in this second group that subsequent flights did not cause such unpleasant sensations; the organism adapted itself to weightlessness.

In the third group are those in whom spatial disorientation takes a more severe expression, lasts for the entire period of weightlessness, and is sometimes accompanied by rapid development of the symptoms of seasickness. Sometimes the illusion of falling is so severe they become terrified, their motor activity becomes abnormal, and they completely lose their ability to get their bearings in space. This psychic reaction is similar to the so-called "end of the world" complex typical of certain mental illnesses and has been described by Dr. A. S. Shmaryan.

> S.'s illness began with a severe headache and dizziness. The patient would experience a sharp falling sensation. His surroundings would change in size and outline, houses would grow larger then

smaller, things would grow dark, buildings would cave in on one another, and everything would become strange and unfamiliar. It would all happen very rapidly. Then it would seem to the patient that tall trees were being torn up by the roots, "that the Earth was a great bubbling caldron, an erupting volcano. Nature, mankind destroyed in a worldwide catastrophe." At these times S. would become afraid, anguished, alarmed; he would sob that he was ready to die. The state would last one or two minutes.

Here are some observations of a man in a state of temporary weightlessness:

Before the onset of weightlessness he sat calmly chatting with the doctor. From the first seconds of weightlessness, there was motor excitement accompanied by snatching motions, involuntary inarticulate cries, a curious facial expression (raised eyebrows, pupils dilated, mouth open, lower jaw slack). The reaction continued for the duration of the period of weightlessness preventing the doctor from making any contact with him. The reaction disappeared with the disappearance of weightlessness but the subject remained in a state of excitement until the end of the flight.

Later the subject himself described his emotions: "I did not realize that I'd gone weightless. I just suddenly felt myself falling and it seemed that everything around me was shattering and going to pieces. I was terrified. I didn't know what was going on." He remembered nothing of his reactions and when he saw a film showing how he had behaved he was extremely surprised.

In space psychology much attention has been given to psychiatric patients whose main symptom is a sensation of a loss of bodily weight. Such patients claim they can walk or swim in air, that they have no feeling in their bodies, that their bodies are "light as a feather, weightless."

The sensation of a loss of bodily weight can be created by drugs. The Russian psychiatrist Sikorskii observed patients under the influence of hashish, in a state in which they felt weightless and free-floating.

The question then arises whether there are general rules that will help us to understand the mechanism controlling unusual psychic reactions to weightlessness. We know that the "end of the world" complex and a series of similar disorders are caused by the dysfunction of certain systems of the brain and a breakdown in the central nervous system. One of the reasons for the dysfunction is distorted information going to the brain from the sensory organs.

One typical example is Ménière's disease, named after the French doctor who first described it in 1861. Ménière's syndrome makes its appearance in apparently absolutely healthy people with a sudden sensation of a blow on the head. As if struck by lightning, they fall to the ground before they even get the chance to grab on to anything. Their ears start ringing, they become dizzy. Some feel that they are being thrown up into the air, others, that the world is turning horizontally or vertically. They see objects double and disappear; the floor, the ground, the bed move out from underneath them and sink away into nothing. They cannot get their bearings.

In fact, Ménière's disease reflects an increased pressure in the semicircular canals of the inner ear that distorts information going to the brain from the sensory organs. Experiments were run on patients with Ménière's disease in a twilight state of elation; when the inner ear was artificially stimulated, they fell into a severe depression with a sense of catastrophe, the end of the world.

In a state of weightlessness, the mechanical forces of gravity cease to operate on the sensory organs, which affects the interaction between the semicircular canals and the utricle, and as a result the brain receives distorted information.

The information from the skin receptors, the cellular tissues, the blood vessels is also fundamentally changed in a state of weightlessness. A flow of nerve impulses from the muscular system to maintain the body in a vertical position is not required in weightlessness. Just how extraordinary a stimulus weightlessness is can be seen in the electrical activity of the brain. In the men participating in the first experiments with weightlessness, there was a decrease in amplitude and an increase in frequency of electrical activity, showing a general excitement of the central nervous system.

In an individual with well-equilibrated nerve processes, the nervous system adapts quickly and begins to work in response to the changed situation, and he may experience a pleasant soaring sensation and be able to continue functioning. Even when the sensation is unpleasant, he can remain in control of his actions.

Titov for example described his state on one such test as something close to seasickness. His head was spinning and whenever he turned it abruptly, objects in front of him would swim and shimmer. He did not, however, lose his bearings, indicating a strong nervous system and great willpower.

But even pilots with strong nervous systems accustomed to perceptual distortions can lose their bearings and suffer a neurotic emotional reaction in a state of nervous exhaustion. This is why it is necessary to study the effect of weightlessness on psychic-physiological mechanisms even more profoundly, and to select the cosmonauts who train for prolonged weightlessness on distant space flights ever more carefully.

Tracks on the Moon

When controlling a spacecraft and making maneuvers and repairs in space, the cosmonaut has to deal in an accurate and coordinated way with levers, buttons, tools. How does space affect his coordination?

Under conditions of temporary weightlessness, men

were given the simple task of hitting an ordinary rifle practice target, placed at arm's length, with a pencil point. The results were not distinguished by their accuracy. With repetition, however, the men became more accurate and the number of bull's-eyes increased.

What happens to destroy coordination? Lifting an arm or leg on Earth, we must overcome the weight and inertia of mass by means of muscle power. In weightlessness, though only an insignificant force is required to move the extremities, the nerve centers still send out strong impulses to the muscles and as a result, the actual motion is in excess of what is required and the hand misses the target.

A special instrument—the coordinograph—has been developed to study coordination. Experiments were run during an ordinary flight in a condition of weightlessness, and they showed that in the majority of cosmonauts the speed of motion slowed down. Popovich, for example, noted in his report: "It was very easy to score on the coordinograph with a slow motion, but rapid motions were hard; the body kept shifting position."

To control a spacecraft and its systems successfully, certain movements must be steady and precise, and here there were more difficulties. In one series of experiments the cosmonauts learned to exert a pressure of 1½ pounds, within less than ½ ounce. In their reports they noted feeling no difference in working the lever under conditions of gravity and conditions of weightlessness, but a film showed that in fact their accuracy was substantially affected by weightlessness: they'd gone over the mark by anywhere from 9 to 40 ounces. Bykovskii went over by only 2 ounces. In subsequent tests the number of errors gradually dropped until by the fifth test there were no substantial errors.

The ground training devices quickly accustomed the cosmonauts to weightlessness. Even in the first space flight, with all that had to be done, Gagarin noticed no loss of coordination, though he experienced some discomfort as a result of the absence of pressure of the chair on his body.

The work of the cosmonauts grew more difficult with each test. They studied the stars, the polar aurora, the surface of the Earth. They measured the height of the stars over the visible horizon, tested the stability of gas bubbles in liquid and water bubbles in gas, took pictures, conducted medical tests and other experiments. And they said that all the small hand movements (pressing levers and telegraph keys, controlling the craft) were made easily and with satisfactory coordination.

What about something requiring more delicate motor coordination—a pencil for example? The reports written by the cosmonauts on test flights show that handwriting coordination was adversely affected. The letters are uneven, the stroke wavering, the ovals angular—testifying to insufficient coordination of movement in the forearm and shoulders with the smaller motions in the hands and fingers.

Handwriting was most adversely affected at the beginning of the flight; on subsequent orbits coordination of the many small motions improved and returned, but never to the normal level.

The improvement in delicate motor coordination during the flight period testifies to man's ability to adapt to unusual conditions. Adaptations can be seen in the handwriting: the letters are shaped more simply, the grip on the pencil and paper becomes tighter, words and symbols that ordinarily would be written separately are now joined by barely visible strokes. Thus we can say that in prolonged periods of weightlessness the adaptations will basically be simplification and increased force of movement.

As men continue to conquer space they will encounter not only weightlessness but unusual gravity forces. Let us say that a man weighing 154 pounds on Earth will weigh 26 pounds on the Moon, but his muscle power will remain the same. If you do not count the space suit this means that man on the Moon will be able to jump six times higher and farther than on Earth because the force of contact with the lunar surface is significantly lessened. Tsiolkovskii imagined the movements of the first man on the Moon this way: "The Russian takes great running leaps, 10 feet up into the air, 40 feet long ... kicking up stones that rise six times higher than on Earth and take a tediously long time to come back down. ... 'I feel so light, it's as if I were up to my neck in water, my feet barely touching the ground. ... I can't resist the temptation, I jump. ... I go up slowly and come down slowly.'" Will the cosmonauts actually be able to coordinate their first steps on the Moon as well as Tsiolkovskii imagined they could?

Some interesting experiments were made in conditions simulating the gravity of the Moon, and it became clear that while swift motion led to a loss of equilibrium and falling, slow motion caused no particular difficulties. It was also discovered that men could make forward and backward somersaults that only gymnasts and acrobats can make on Earth.

One of the subjects described his feelings:

> First step. Probably I put too much into it. I soar up into the air and come down several meters from the starting line nowhere near where I intended, my legs dangling helplessly. Another push and the same thing happens. . . . I try to run but can't. I kick my legs hard and fall. It is like suddenly falling on ice: the harder I try to get my legs together, the harder it is to get my balance. . . . I try making little jumps slightly sideways. It's easier to keep my balance. Strange as it may seem, you can't go faster than 0.6 mile per hour on the Moon, 50 feet per minute, because after lifting up from the surface you come down much slower than on Earth. . . . I tried jumping on a "rock" (as the subject imagined a bench). I got one foot on, but not the other. I fell over it and after hanging for a bit in an intricate pose I landed a yard away.

A simulation of lunar gravity does not give a true picture, but even on the basis of these imperfect experiments we can draw one preliminary conclusion: man's coordination on the Moon will differ both from his coordination on Earth and in weightlessness. Better training devices must be developed to simulate the reduced gravity of the Moon (one-sixth of Earth's gravity) and help the cosmonauts to adjust more quickly to conditions on the lunar surface.

Without plane of reference

Few men as yet have walked in space. But the time is not distant when the cosmonauts will be leaving the spacecraft and going out into open space more and more often to dock in space and transfer from one craft to another. What will the psychic-physiological reactions be?

No matter what man is doing, he always has a plane of reference. The slightest motion or change of attitude changes the center of gravity in relation to the reference plane and equilibrium is restored by a compensatory movement (a twist of the body, a thrust of the hand). When walking, for example, a man actively changes the center of gravity in relation to his reference plane, "catching at it" with his forward foot. He then maintains equilibrium and stability by choosing the optimal rhythm of motion.

Even when a man is standing still, though he is usually unaware of it, the muscles are constantly working to maintain equilibrium, and the smaller the reference plane, the harder they must work. When an immediate response to a loss of equilibrium is required, the signals go out automatically. The body has only to slip and start to fall before it leans automatically in the opposite direction, the center of gravity shifts, and equilibrium is restored. One or another group of muscles is at work before a man knows what is happening.

Cats are particularly good at maintaining a certain

position in relation to their plane of reference: falling upside down from a height of a yard, they manage to land on their feet.

The Dutch scientist Magnus first discovered the physiological mechanism involved in the control of position. He proved that the ability of men and animals to achieve equilibrium in space is due to complex combined processes in the nuclei of the medulla, cerebellum, and cortex that are constantly processing information coming in from sensory organs, vestibular nerve, muscles, and other organs. Magnus proved that impulses from the utricle of the inner ear determine the position of the cat's head during a fall. The whole chain of reflexes can be visualized thus: Signals from the utricle orient the cat's head in a certain relation to the force of gravity, which in turn leads to a shift in position of the torso and extremities. It is a chain reaction to the force of gravity and it operates fast and accurately.

We have been speaking of the reaction of men and animals to a loss of equilibrium and a plane of reference in terms of fractions of seconds, a phenomenon familiar to anyone who has gone down in an express elevator and had the unpleasant sensation that the floor (the reference plane) is dropping away under his feet. But scientists are interested in what happens in prolonged loss of reference plane, in the condition of weightlessness.

In the first high-altitude rockets, mice and rats were sent up in special cages equipped with cameras. With the onset of weightlessness the rats and mice rolled around aimlessly, vainly trying to stop themselves. The movements of their paws and tails sent them spinning harder and turning somersaults. But there were differences in how the different animals adjusted to weightlessness. With the white mice the speed of rotation did not change during the entire period of weightlessness, while the rats grew accustomed to their new state—they spread their paws apart and tried to hook their tails to the sides of the cage.

Other animals reacted differently. At the onset of weightlessness rabbits would make a series of movements rather like jumps, and then begin drumming their front paws. As they became accustomed to weightlessness they would tuck themselves up stretching out their front paws, and finally they would float free, paws crossed.

Cats reacted more individually. Some would mew loudly and wave their paws, eyes wide open; others would try to grab at anything within reach. Dogs, their eyes popping with fear, would paw the air and their tails would vibrate at first; but later they would calm down more than any other animal, and settle themselves quite comfortably in midair.

The fact that these reactions were caused by distorted information passing from the utricle to the brain was proved by the following experiment. The utricle in some turtles and white mice was surgically destroyed. In the first days after the operation they were completely disoriented, and unable to coordinate their movements. After several days, however, thanks to eyesight, coordination began to return. When they were put into a state of weightlessness, it was much easier for them to orient themselves and coordinate their movements than it was for the control animals who had not undergone the operation. The latter, as a result of the sudden loss of information from the inner ear, displayed complete disorientation and chaotic motor reactions.

When first tested in the weightlessness pool men lose all ability to control their motions. At the onset of weightlessness they instinctively begin to make swimming motions with their arms and legs. They resemble people who don't know how to swim floundering about in the water.

In subsequent tests their aimless movements become coordinated. If at first the cosmonauts tended to fly from side to side of the pool, later they learned how to hold their bodies and move about in space.

During one test Nikolaev and Popovich freed

themselves of the tether and discovered the tendency of the body to move toward the "ceiling," an effect caused in all probability by the rotation of the spacecraft, which, though very slow, is enough to create a slight centrifugal force.

It must be emphasized that in these tests the cosmonauts were not totally without a reference plane. They were in a space laboratory or the cabin of a plane and always had something to swim toward, bump against, and give them new direction. It was an essentially new and much more difficult task that confronted Aleksei Leonov on his space walk. He had to orient himself in "pure" space, almost totally without a reference plane.

We have said that in the future men are going to have to work in open space, but any work operation calls for an exertion that can throw the cosmonaut. That was why Leonov rehearsed all his movements in the space laboratory on a mock-up of the Voskhod-2 equipped with an actual-size hatch. The main flight assignment—the walk in space—was rehearsed in a series of consecutive operations. First the cosmonaut had to don the life-support system and get it going. He checked all the equipment involved in the space walk and adjusted the pressure in the hatch chamber. He moved to the hatch chamber where he checked the pressure in his helmet and suit, the windows in the helmet, the oxygen-feed system. The captain of the craft closed off the cabin, depressurized the hatch chamber, and opened the hatch. The cosmonaut executed the scheduled number of exits from and returns to the hatch, and finally returned to the cabin.

So long as he was in his chair, in one fixed spot, it was easy for the cosmonaut to work accurately. It became more difficult when he had to move about inside the cabin or hatch and infinitely more so in open space. His success depended on how well he judged the force of his push-off from the spacecraft. It had to be an energetic one, even though he might hit something, in order to get through the hatch fast enough. Hampered by his space suit and a weak push, he might not make it at all.

The skills involved in exits from and returns to the spacecraft had to be worked out slowly. At first movements were abrupt with the body rotating horizontally and vertically. The exercise of moving smoothly away from and toward the spacecraft had to be practiced over and over.

In his report written at the end of his training Leonov wrote: "The test went well. I had no unpleasant feelings, just the same feelings I experienced on earlier weightlessness tests. The space suit hampered me a bit and the helmet restricted my vision. The hatch approaches were easy because by tensing my line I could get my bearings and a sense of direction. The exits and approaches could then be made smoothly. Apparently it is possible to do any kind of work in weightlessness without noticeable loss of coordination."

Leonov left the spacecraft and returned to it five times. He did everything exactly as he had in practice training. Though he was not able to stabilize his body immediately, and rocked back and forth for a while, his organism soon adjusted to the situation, thus confirming the proposition that even in open space a man's coordination and ability to orient himself and work suffer no fundamental damage.

To work and maneuver in space a special "reaction gun" or air gun became necessary. American astronaut Edward White had a 26-foot tether line, two cameras, and a jet-stream oxygen gun on his walk in space.

In search of weight

After a successful 34-hour flight, American astronaut Gordon Cooper looked very pale; he felt weak and his eyes were hollow. His blood pressure had dropped from 120 to 90. The doctors diagnosed his condition as a loss of tone in the veins, due to weight-lessness, hemostasis in the extremities, and blockage of the flow of blood to the heart.

Similar problems have been observed in dogs. Ugolek and Veterok, who were in orbit for 22 days, could scarcely stand on their feet at the end of the flight. There were irregularities in blood vessels and other organs that took a long time to disappear.

On interplanetary flights man will be in a state of weightlessness for many months, years perhaps. Will he be able to control the spacecraft for a landing on a planet where once again the force of gravity will begin to operate? To answer this question we must understand the cause of man's weakness after returning from a state of weightlessness.

Maintenance of a vertical position on Earth demands constant nervous-muscular activity. A significant percentage of our energy is spent simply counteracting gravity. A man living in a spacecraft in a state of weightlessness for a prolonged period of time will suffer from a sharp deterioration of muscle power.

Blood pressure depends on force of the heartbeat, tone of the blood-vessel walls, and weight of the circulating blood, which accounts for 10% to 15% of the total pressure. In a state of weightlessness, when blood weight disappears along with the necessity for muscle power to maintain the body in a vertical position, the stress on the heart and blood vessels is significantly reduced. Muscular inaction of and reduced stress on the heart affect other processes. Nerve impulses flowing from the brain to the muscles are affected, which in turn has its effect on psychic-physiological reactions.

Long-range effects of weightlessness were studied in men immersed in water, because to some extent a pool can simulate the condition of weightlessness in the enclosed space of the spacecraft. The ordinary sense of weight and the muscular activity counteracting gravity are missing.

Tsiolkovskii first suggested the idea in his "Dream

about Earth and Sky": "A man whose average density is equal to the density of water will become as if weightless when immersed in water, although it will be very very far from the full effect."

An experiment involving 27 men has been described in the foreign press. Nine men equipped with air and food stayed underwater for 6, then 12, then 24 hours. Nine others were kept underwater for seven days, coming up to the surface briefly once a day. The rest were immersed in water up to their necks with their heads resting on a spongy pillow and their bodies wrapped in netting. Five of them were in for 5 to 24 hours, the other four for 10 hours a day for 14 days, spending the rest of the time in bed.

The results of this experiment were very interesting. While still in the water all of the subjects reacted against the "freedom" of their condition and experienced the desire to hang on to something. They all complained of feeling weak and were surprised to find that their muscle power had not been affected— the few movements they made were enough to maintain muscle tone during such a relatively short period of reduced gravity. Blood pressure dropped, but pulse and respiration were not fundamentally affected. Coordination was not damaged, though motor responses were slowed down.

When the subjects emerged from the water, many felt weak, with trembling legs; one even lost consciousness. The cardiovascular system seems to have been most noticeably affected. Later, when the subjects were put in the centrifuge with an acceleration stress of 4 to 5 G's, several lost their vision and others simply couldn't stand the stress at all, although underwater they had had no trouble taking 10 G's.

Something similar happens to people who stay in bed for a long time. All the mechanisms regulating blood pressure for a body in a vertical position are shut off, lowering the hydrostatic pressure. When a man gets up from bed after a long illness, the lowered pressure in his cardiovascular system makes itself felt in dizziness and a tendency to lose consciousness. Prolonged inactivity also weakens muscle tone and can eventually lead to muscular atrophy.

It is clear then that unless measures are taken, blood circulation and in time muscle tone will be damaged on an interplanetary flight. This, in turn, will affect nervous-psychic processes after landing on Earth or another planet where the force of gravity operates.

How can cosmonauts be protected from these dangers? The first thought—one that also occurred to Tsiolkovskii—is the creation of an artificial field of gravity by rotating the spacecraft. We know from physics that the weight of a rotating body depends on the velocity and radius of the rotation. A simple calculation will show that in order to create a force of gravity equal to that on Earth the rotating spacecraft must have a radius of several hundred meters—if less than that, the speed of rotation would have to be increased to a dangerous level.

We now feel that the artificial gravity on an interplanetary flight does not have to correspond to gravity on Earth; it can be several times less. Men and objects will still have weight, there will be an up and a down.

Another answer is constant physical exercise with springs and rubber pulleys that require the same muscle power in weightlessness as on Earth. In one experiment five men were confined for two weeks in bed; three of them did daily exercises to keep up muscle tone, the other two did not. At the end of the experiment, the damage to the cardiovascular system in all five men was identical.

Experiments performed with men immersed in water provided the same results. Physical exercise helped preserve muscle tone but could do nothing to offset the influence of the reduced gravity or to strengthen the cardiovascular system.

In another experiment a man was lowered into a pool dressed in a special suit with pneumatic cuffs that cut off the circulation in the extremities. During the course of the experiment the cuffs were periodically inflated for 60 seconds to a pressure of 2.4 inches on the mercury column. The inflated cuffs increased the circulation in the extremities by keeping the blood circulation mechanisms stimulated. In the opinion of those running the experiment, the inflated cuffs simulated the hydrostatic effect of the vertical position. At the end of the experiment the blood pressure, heartbeat, and electrocardiograph readings were all identical with the control readings taken before the experiment. Pneumatic cuffs were used by Gordon Cooper during the eight-day flight of Gemini-5.

American scientists have proposed building a special compartment for a centrifuge in an orbital station to cope with the blood-circulation problem before returning to Earth. By means of artificial gravity, physical exercise, special suits, and the centrifuge, cosmonauts can in all probability be protected from the harmful effects of weightlessness on long space flights.

CHAPTER SEVEN

Secrets of Silence

Nearly 30% of all pilots who mount to an altitude of 10 to 15 kilometers in planes or balloons begin to feel cut off from the Earth, and their reactions to this feeling fall in two opposing categories. Half of them find it very pleasant; they experience a joyous excitement and a great desire to prolong the flight as long as possible. The other half find it difficult and terrifying. These pilots confess to a "feeling of alienation from my own body, as if it were somewhere else," and to aural and visual hallucinations.

Such phenomena have been explained by psychologists as sensory starvation, the reaction of the human psyche to a monotony of impressions, an insufficient number of outside stimuli, of which we spoke at the beginning of the book. It is a problem that had to be dealt with when men began training for the first space flights.

In tests abroad, in order that they might be fully insulated from the outside world, men were put into special boxes equipped with couches. Their eyes were covered with opaque glasses, their ears covered with earphones that cut off all sound—even that of their own voices—and their hands were covered with gloves that prevented any tactile sensation.

The men quickly began to feel "starved" for outside impressions. To satisfy their need some tried knocking on the wall of the box. They were oppressed by not having any clear idea whether they were awake or asleep. The majority refused to go on with the experiment after 24 to 72 hours, and those who stayed more than two days suffered from hallucinations.

In another series of tests men were immersed in a specially equipped pool of water where they were cut off not only from light and sound but also from any sense of fulcrum or surface. The temperature was held constant. In the first hours the subjects thought about the events of the passing day, about themselves or their families. Then came a strange feeling of satisfaction that quickly changed to anxiety. Experiencing a sharper and sharper need for outside stimuli they began flexing their muscles, making swimming motions, tapping their fingers together. If they were left in the water, eventually their attention turned completely inward. They would lose all sense of time and begin to have wild fantasies and hallucinations, both aural and visual.

Floating there in the water, many distinctly heard the buzzing of bees, birdcalls, human voices, music. Others saw light flares, geometric figures, whole little scenes. One saw a line of squirrels marching over the snow with bags over their shoulders. Others saw basketball games and other sports events, drops of water falling from a ceiling. There was a sense of bodily dislocation, the separation of the head and arms from the body.

Scientists abroad had to handle many psychic disturbances in tests conducted in mock-up spacecraft with the subject working alone. In one such test the assignment was to keep "Earth" informed of bodily temperature, humidity and air pressure in the cabin, readings on the various instruments, and also to follow the television-transmitted signals on the automatic controls. Whenever the television signals disappeared the man in the cabin was supposed to take over the manual controls.

This is seemingly a perfectly harmless situation. But one highly qualified pilot became very dizzy, though the craft had not moved at all. For another pilot unfamiliar faces began to appear among the instruments on the control panel. For a third, the control panel suddenly began to "melt and drip to the floor" as the "flight" came to an end. A fourth complained of pain in his eyes because of the diffusion of images on the television screen, when in fact it was empty. Unconvinced by assurances that nothing had gone wrong, he demanded that the experiment be ended immediately and said when he emerged from the chamber that in addition to the other illusions he had felt the walls closing in on him.

In one case a subject asked that the television be turned off after 22 hours because he claimed it was producing unbearable heat. No matter what the doctor said, the pilot insisted that it be turned off and when it was, he immediately began to feel better. It was then turned on again and within three hours the same scene was repeated again. This time the pilot found a reason for the heat, pointing to a "black burned-out spot" on the screen and demanded to be "freed" as he could no longer take it.

There are many such examples—persuasive evidence that absolute silence and solitude are a great threat to the psychic state of man.

At the helm of a caravel

Hallucinations are often called sensory deceptions. They have no concrete outside stimulus and can be false images, sounds, or other sense impressions. Hallucinations produce the effect of reality and arouse a corresponding reaction: a man answers voices, defends himself from approaching danger. They may also take completely fantastic forms, but in either case, those suffering hallucinations are firmly convinced of the reality of their perceptions.

Even before the space flights we were of the opinion that a dearth of outside stimuli would have its effect on the normal human psyche, and the experiments conducted in isolation chambers showed that while a healthy man with a strong nervous system could sustain prolonged isolation and remain able to work without permanent psychic damage, he indeed experienced unusual, though not unhealthy, psychic phenomena.

Dr. V. Lebedev and Dr. O. Kuznetsov conducted one 10-to-14-day experiment in an isolation chamber that was designed to study work capacity and the dynamics of physiological and psychic processes during various patterns of sleep, work, and rest. The subjects, like the cosmonauts, were all between 20 and 30 years of age. An electroencephalograph and other instruments recording physiological functions were used and highly sensitive microphones were placed around the chamber.

Various muffled sounds were transmitted to subject S. in the isolation chamber and his job was to identify them. In the cases where S. knew what was going on outside the chamber he could identify the noises and conversations fairly accurately, but when he did not know, he made mistakes. He misunderstood conversations, failed to recognize voices, and once identified the noises in the engine room as a record by the popular singer Robertino Loretti. S. had no doubts about what he had heard.

His was a sensory deception caused by extreme dearth of incoming stimuli, similar to the illusions experienced in actual space practice. The American astronaut Gordon Cooper said that when he was flying over Tibet he could see with the naked eye houses and other buildings through the spacecraft window. But according to all calculations, the human eye is incapable of perceiving such objects from such an altitude. At first the American experts deemed the phenomenon a hallucination caused by solitude and sensory starvation, but later, during a discussion of this question at a congress on aviation and space medicine, they agreed with Soviet experts that what had been involved was not a hallucination but an illusion.

Though we often speak of sensory deceptions, in the proper sense of the words, they do not exist. In the 18th century the philosopher Immanuel Kant wrote that "our senses do not deceive us, not because they always judge correctly, but because they don't judge at all." Experiments have proved that the greater part of sensory deceptions are caused by the fact that we unconsciously make ourselves see what we see. "We see with our brains, not our eyes," say the psychologists. We involuntarily lead ourselves astray, and it is our judgments, not our senses, that deceive us. The example of S. is convincing proof: it was a misunderstanding that led to his sensory deception, an illusion of recognition.

In the conditions of solitude a false recognition is not necessarily an illusion, rather the most probable hypothesis to explain an unknown phenomenon, as in the case of the cosmonaut who mistook the sound of work going on underground not far from the laboratory for the sound of dancing in the next room. However, he, unlike S., was not certain about it.

Similar mistakes are not in themselves signs of mental illness. But if the healthy man does suffer from illusions, his psychic state of fatigue, distraction, expectation, and fear is of great importance. It is to the naturally timid and fearful, particularly in solitude, that night brings its horrors and specters.

A subject of one of the experiments said that on the tenth day he had the strange feeling that there was some formless person standing behind his chair in the chamber. He couldn't make out whether it was a man or woman, old or young. In the given instance, the perception was based on no visual or aural sensation. He knew perfectly well there was no one in the chamber, yet he could not rid himself of the unpleasant feeling. Logically, his only explanation was that that day he had been tense and unable to occupy himself during the unscheduled hours.

The physical cause might have been the ventilation system located right behind his chair. Under normal conditions he would never have noticed the small changes in pressure and temperature, but in prolonged isolation, with a dearth of stimuli, the sensitivity of the skin increased to the point where he sensed a non-existent presence.

Other writings by James and Jepps have confirmed this hypothesis explaining the "presence" of an outsider in an isolation chamber. James has described the "consciousness of presence" in a certain blind man. Like many blind men his auditory and tactile senses were highly developed. By signs undiscernible to others—barely perceptible air currents, the slightest temperature changes, acoustical vibrations—he could sense the appearance and approach of another person. Sometimes, sitting down at a piano in silence, the blind man would get the sense of a man slipping through the half-open door and lying on the couch behind him. But when he began to play or talk, the figure would disappear.

Jepps made an analogous observation of a man with normal vision who pointed out that the flow of air coming in from the door was responsible for a false sense of presence. A similar phenomenon is particularly well described in a book by the American mariner Joshua Slocum, who circumnavigated the Earth in the small yacht *Spree* at the end of the last century. Starting out on April 24, 1895, he completed his voyage July 27, 1897, having sailed 46,000 miles.

One day the courageous sailor got sick on goat cheese and could not handle the boat. He lashed the helm and lay down in the cabin. Slocum wrote:

> When I came to, I saw that the *Spree* was in stormy waters. Looking up, to my amazement I saw a tall man at the helm holding the wheel in a strong, almost vicelike grip. You can imagine my surprise. He was dressed like a foreign sailor—a cock's comb was hanging over his left ear from his broad red cap and his face was framed by thick black side-whiskers. He could have been taken for a pirate anywhere in the world. Faced with this frightening appearance, I forgot about the stern

and could only think about whether or not the stranger was going to slit my throat. He appeared to guess my thoughts. "Señor," he said, raising his cap, "I intend you no harm." A faint smile played on his face, which immediately became more pleasant. "I'm a volunteer from Columbus' crew and am guilty of nothing. . . . I'm the helmsman of the *Pinta* and have come to help you. . . . Lie down, Señor Capitan, and I'll steer your boat all night."

I wondered what the devil he was doing sailing full sail, and as if he'd guessed my thoughts, he exclaimed, "The *Pinta*'s up ahead and we have to overtake her. We have to go full speed ahead, full speed!"

V. I. Myasnikov has described the vivid visual and aural perceptions of a correspondent kept in an isolation chamber without a watch or any other way to mark off the day. He was told he could eat and sleep whenever he pleased.

On the fourth day the correspondent began to hear snatches of music. He wrote in his diary:

So how do I feel? At times satisfied, at other times miserable. I have some kind of an inner tension that keeps me listening all the time, and it's good to remember melodies. Sometimes they just come unbidden. I have heard Rachmaninoff's Preludes, Brahms, Ravel's Concerto for Violin and Orchestra, and of course the great Beethoven. I haven't heard such pure Beethoven in a long time. I lie around "in the morning," too lazy to get up, with Beethoven's Ninth, in a German rendition, in my ears, and it's unutterably pleasurable. Listening to Rachmaninoff, I suddenly saw the Great Hall in the Conservatory and even heard the voice of the woman announcer. Plays come even easier, and beloved arias, songs, boring scraps of dance music keep going around. Haunting. The only way to escape is to listen to what sounds there are inside the chamber and all my inner music turns off.

Characteristic of these phenomena are the side effects, the associations made in the consciousness. A television apparatus turned on suddenly frightened the correspondent and gave rise to an unexpected association. "Forestry in the Carpathians. A man crushed by a falling tree. Astonished by the clarity of the sounds, the saw, the crack of the falling tree."

Associations such as these, made in isolation, have a convincing reality, but in contradistinction to hallucinations can usually be recognized as the fruit of imagination and dismissed as such. They are "eidetic" phenomena.

Eidetic imagery is common in childhood. Children not only imagine objects, they actually visualize objects they remember. One boy of 13 has said, "As soon as I think of something, I see it." Eidetic imagery is not limited to children; in adults it seems to be a precondition for art. A. N. Tolstoy wrote of his heroes: "I could actually see them." Another Russian author, I. A. Goncharov, wrote: "My characters give me no peace, they get up, strike poses. I listen to segments of their conversation and it often seems to me that I'm not making this up, it's all floating in the air around me and I have only to watch and to listen."

Gustave Flaubert not only distinctly saw his heroes, he lived with them. In 1870 he wrote in one of his letters, "When I described the death of Emma Bovary I had such a taste of arsenic in my mouth and became so nauseated that after my meal I vomited."

The 18th-century painter Joshua Reynolds painted his portraits in the following way. There would be the usual first sitting: the subject would sit in a chair and Reynolds would make a sketch for about 30 or 40 minutes. After that the subject was no longer needed. Relying on the extraordinary power of his memory he could place the chair in the same spot near the easel and summon the image of his subject as if she were actually sitting in front of him. The work would go as well as at the first sitting, the portrait would take shape. If someone happened to step between him and the empty chair Reynolds would ask him to step aside and not block the woman.

The psychic effect of eidetic phenomena has forced some richly gifted artists to take self-protective measures. Beethoven for example used to douse himself in cold water. E. T. W. Hoffmann, when frightened by his heroes, would ask his wife to come sit beside him.

Boys' choir

In one test conducted in the isolation chamber the doctor on duty turned the lights on 20 minutes after lights out. Subject P. reported the fact in his morning report. Three days later he reported that the lights the night before had gone on at the wrong time; but in fact they had not. It must have been a dream but it was taken for reality.

Similar phenomena are of course possible in an ordinary situation. Here is an excerpt from the diary of Professor Maiorov, a specialist on dream theory. "Just before dawn, in a vague semiwaking state, I suddenly thought that Nanny should be coming in soon. Then I fell asleep and saw her crossing from the table to the dresser. I woke up and the dream had been so vivid that I checked to see if she had really come or not. There was no one there. She hadn't come after all."

Children often confuse dreams with reality. So do primitive, superstitious peoples on a low level of civilization. A European traveling in Africa was once approached by a native living over 60 miles away and told, "You must pay me a fine." "What for?" "I dreamed you killed my slave." Despite many protests that he could not have killed the slave because he had never been in that area, the traveler paid the fine.

Another observer has told the story of the American Indian coming to him and demanding payment for three stolen pumpkins. Proof? The Indian had seen him stealing the pumpkins in a dream and that was proof enough.

A third observer has told of staying in a home where the host tore out on the street in the middle of the night and started shooting because he had dreamed that someone was shooting his neighbor.

Prolonged isolation, when a man has no way to check on himself by checking with other people, can create a situation where the line between dream and reality is almost completely erased. Let us open the diary of another subject in an isolation chamber. "While writing out my medical reports on December 24, at 1:30 in the afternoon, it seems I fell asleep. In my sleep I saw Edik come in. Or did I? It was Tuesday and Rostislav Borisovich was the doctor on duty. I got on the radio and asked him to say hello to Edik. That was to check."

One can assume that there was no Edik in the laboratory at the time, since the electroencephalograph readings show a typical dream pattern. It is curious, however, that the subject was uncertain whether his comrade had actually entered the isolation chamber and that he developed such a great need to find out if it had been dream or reality.

The electroencephalograph shows us that in a state of solitude the cortex of the brain enters a hypnotic state, halfway between sleeping and waking. The first phase of the hypnotic state is what Pavlov called the equalization phase, one in which strong and weak stimuli evoke an identical reaction from the organism, whereas in the waking state the strong stimulus evokes a more energetic response. This is followed by the paradoxical phase, in which the weak stimulus evokes a strong response. Then there is the third or ultraparadoxical phase, in which a positive stimulus that ordinarily arouses an excited response arouses an inhibitory response and vice versa. Finally there is the state of total inhibition, in which the organism ceases to respond to ordinary stimuli at all.

When the subject is awakened, these phases are repeated in reverse order and in quick succession as a rule, and in these shifting, partially sleeping states, illusions are fairly frequent. One of Pavlov's assistants, Dr. Maiorov, made these observations of himself:

1st observation: I woke up around seven and opened my eyes. It was dusk. The back of the dresser standing by the bed looked like two giant outstretched gloved hands. When the illusion disappeared, it was actually a towel hanging from the dresser and two boxes sitting on top. The illusion came during a shifting phase of partial sleep, when the cortex was in a state of inhibition.

2nd observation: A bust of Leo Tolstoy stands at the window, face turned in toward the room. In the morning light, when I wake up, it always looks different to me.

3rd observation: One morning I woke up early and was amazed to see a girl standing by the mirror. I looked carefully and the illusion disappeared: a woman's jacket and hat were hanging on a tall stool and I had taken the stool legs for a girl's legs.

Dr. S. Bugrov experienced a number of interesting states during his prolonged stay in isolation. Here are excerpts from his diary:

Today I want to set down a fairly interesting phenomenon that I experienced a few nights ago before falling asleep but didn't get into the diary right away so I forgot it till now. Just before falling asleep I began to hear music. I was frightened when I first heard it, remembering the aural hallucinations connected with schizophrenia. I remembered my first patient in Professor Kutanin's clinic. He was the first violinist at the ballet. Aside from the basic symptom—a split personality—he had extremely strong aural hallucinations. But he was a highly trained musician (he graduated from the Saratov and Moscow conservatories), I'm not. I was quite worried.

Just as I was sinking into deep sleep, I heard the music again. Now I began to listen to it more carefully. It was a mournful but pleasant melody, much like Japanese music, which rose to the very highest notes, then dropped to the very lowest. It was unearthly somehow, similar to the music we associate with space and spectrums and gamma rays. But I found it very pleasant.

I don't remember the further course of events as I fell asleep. There were no dreams connected with the music, no dreams at all. I woke up and forgot all about it. The next time I heard music it was like organ music played in a hall with good acoustics. Again the music ranged from low to high tones. The melody was majestic and touched me very very deeply—I was reminded of the most important moments in my life—and the leitmotiv was one of mild sadness, possibly because it was organ music, which tends to be sad and somewhat mystical. One thing I can say, it was very pleasant and it touched off associations hard to convey. Again there were no dreams particularly connected with the music. I did have one short dream about my daughter, but that's a dream I have frequently.

Another time the organ music was joined by a boys' choir singing in high, melodic, almost squeaky tones. I don't much like boys' voices, frankly; Sveshnikov's Boys' Choir has always struck me as inferior. But this time the music aroused most positive emotions, I wanted to listen and listen and listen. But my pleasure must have been interrupted by sleep, and again there were no dreams. This was repeated several more times.

What was it? The fruit of a sick fantasy or objective reality transformed into music? I cannot say. I can only say that these phenomena all could have been connected to the ventilator. But why only at night, before sleep, and not during the day? And a second thing, why was it a different kind of music each time? The acoustics in the chamber? Silly to even talk about acoustics, in my opinion. What kind of acoustics in the musical sense can you have in a vault? I'm not going to

rack my brains over this—I'll try and get the psychologists and acoustical engineers to explain it.
I must stop now or I'll have visual hallucinations
as well, always thinking about the same thing.

The musical hallucinations, as we saw, developed
slowly over the course of prolonged isolation and
came only at a time when the noise of the ventilator
was interfering with the process of falling asleep.
Later as the noise gradually diminished, subjectively
speaking, the subject began to fall asleep more quickly
and easily.

Explaining similar phenomena in terms of hypnosis,
Pavlov once wrote:

> Our general concept of opposites is one of the most
> basic and necessary of our concepts, a concept
> that helps make normal thought processes and
> other general concepts possible. Our relation to
> our environment, to the social sphere, and to our-
> selves is inevitably going to be highly distorted if
> opposites are constantly confused: I–not I, mine–
> yours, I alone–I in society, I that am doing harm–
> I that am being harmed, etc. There has to be a
> very profound cause for the disappearance or de-
> terioration of this general concept and that cause
> must be sought, in my opinion, in the basic laws of
> the nervous system. I think physiology already has
> the answers. . . .
> What then is the analysis of this deterioration
> as a nervous phenomenon? Here we have several
> separate physiological factors. The foundation for
> the analysis is provided first of all by the peripheral
> endings of all the afferent nervous conductors of
> the organism, each of which is specially adjusted
> to transform a definite kind of energy (both inside
> and outside the organism) in the process of ner-
> vous excitation; this process is then conducted to
> special, less numerous cells of the lower parts of
> the central nervous system, as well as to the highly
> numerous special cells of the cerebral hemisphere.

From there, however, the process of nervous excitation usually irradiates to various cells over a
greater or lesser area. . . . Afterward the irradiation
gradually becomes more and more limited; the
excitatory process concentrates in the smallest nervous process as inhibition. . . .

Along with the law of irradiation and concentration of the nervous processes, there is another
permanently operating fundamental law—the law
of reciprocal induction. According to this law, the
effect of the positive conditioned stimulus becomes
stronger when the latter is applied immediately or
shortly after the concentrated inhibitory stimulus,
just as the effect of the inhibitory stimulus proves
to be more exact and profound after the concentrated positive stimulus. . . .

The entire establishment and distribution in the
cortex of excitatory and inhibitory states, taking
place in a certain period under the action of external and internal stimuli, becomes more and more
fixed under uniform, recurring conditions and is
effected with ever-increasing ease and automatism.
Thus there appears a dynamic stereotype (systematization) in the cortex. . . .

After a conditioned stimulus applied during a
certain period of time, we put food before the
dog who turns away from the food receptacle. But
when we begin to move the receptacle away, the
dog makes a movement in its direction. We present
the receptacle anew; the dog turns toward it once
more. We have termed the reaction of turning away
from the food . . . the first phase of negativism or
contralism. The negativism may recur many times
until the animal at last partakes of the food, which
happens in most cases. The degree of hypnosis is
expressed precisely by the number of repetitions of
this procedure.

That Bugrov's hypnotic music took place during the
ultraparadoxical phase is clear from the most interesting excerpt in his diary. "Again, music before falling
asleep. It was the sounds of a bugle turned into pleasant music. Then sleep." Bugrov could not explain the

sudden appearance of the bugle, but later it became clear. The fact was that school had started on September 1 but Bugrov's daughter had had to miss school on account of a serious illness. The thought of her had not left him all day. Dropping off to sleep, he tried to rid himself of his worries but they found their expression by association with the school band in that bugle music.

During the ultraparadoxical phase relatively stable emotional attitudes worked out over the course of a lifetime toward objects and phenomena in the outside world can be broken down. Ideas lose their usual associations and the emotional reaction can be the exact opposite of the usual reaction. The following excerpt from a diary kept in an isolation chamber is further testimony: "I'm going back to sleep. The strange business with the hallucinations (I can't call them anything else) is still going on. Falling asleep yesterday I heard an organ playing Russian folk songs in such fantastic variations, I couldn't imagine how anyone could think them up. Then it was a song I don't like at all. At the end boys' voices joined in and it was so wonderful, it was simply bliss. Bliss from that song! What's gotten into me?"

As we have said, Bugrov's music developed against the background of the ventilator. At the beginning the noise bothered him and prevented him from sleeping. As he gradually became more accustomed to the monotonous hum, he apparently began to "neutralize" it with his own music. Nothing similar had ever happened to him before. When he had traveled by train, the clack of the wheels had created various rhythmic melodies that he knew to be in his head. In isolation, however, the music seemed to be coming from the outside world.

The illusion is a characteristic "aural eidetic image." Composers are familiar with the phenomenon when in the moment of highest inspiration musical ideas seem to assert themselves independently from the creative mind. Beethoven "heard" his music when he was totally deaf at the end of his life. Gounod said of himself: "I hear my heroes singing as clearly as I see objects around me. It sends me into ecstasy.... I sit for hours listening to my Romeo or Juliet or Friar Laurence or some other character, convinced that I am actually hearing them."

Since these eidetic phenomena have a fully scientific explanation and represent no particular mystery, the cosmonauts will be able to cope with their sensory deceptions during an orbital flight and not be frightened by them. They will know that they can verify anything dubious by radio, obtain supplementary information, and be able to separate the actual from the conjectural and unclear.

De Meran's discovery

In 1729 an astronomer named de Meran, studying the rotation of the Earth upon its axis, made the discovery that plants kept in the dark at a constant temperature exhibited the same periodic movement of leaves as plants kept in conditions of changing light and temperatures. This fact drew the attention of researchers, many experiments were made on various organisms, and it became clear that even the simplest organisms kept in conditions of constant light (or darkness) will retain a balanced rhythm of activity, calm, growth, and cell division in any 24-hour cycle. This rhythm was called the circadian rhythm.

A series of experiments were made on squirrels. A squirrel placed in a cage equipped with a meter for measuring revolutions was kept in total darkness for several months. The meter showed that the squirrel came to life every evening. The cage would begin to turn again after an identical period of time, approximately equal to a day.

Experiments with six generations of mice kept constantly in the light showed that their repeated pattern of physiological functions (periods of activity, sleep, and wakefulness) approximated a circadian rhythm.

There has been great scientific interest in the teams working in the Arctic where the Sun does not rise and set daily. Research done in Spitsbergen showed that uninterrupted daylight over a period of two months had no noticeable effect on the physiological processes of people from the central latitudes.

According to contemporary scientific understanding all plants and animals kept in constant conditions will maintain a circadian physiological rhythm that is connected to the existence in all organisms of "biological time." The regulation of physiological processes in unicellular organisms and plants is apparently biochemical, and the rhythm is worked out by a process of adaptation to the periodicity of night and day on the planet. The reader will find further interesting material in a book on biological time by A. M. Aime.

The German scientist G. Klug proved that in invertebrates the circadian rhythm is regulated by the nervous system. The British scientist Janet Harker, experimenting with the cockroach, a typical nighttime creature, discovered that a ganglion in the neck gives off chemical substances that regulate its biological rhythm. In one experiment a cockroach was kept in the light until it had lost any distinct rhythm of motor activity and then its ganglion was removed and replaced with the ganglion of a normal cockroach. Within a few days the rhythm of motor activity had been restored.

The higher animals have more complex mechanisms regulating circadian rhythm. There are the relatively simple regulators involved in respiration and oxidation and the more complex processes coordinated by the brain. If the cortex is removed, the diurnal pattern of sleeping and waking remains, as do the daily fluctuation of bodily temperatures, respiration and oxidation, pulse rate, blood pressure, and other functions, which means that the biological regulators must be located below the cortex, in the medulla. This does not mean, however, that the cortex is in no way involved in the regulation of physiological functions; it is the activity of this layer of gray matter investing the surface of the cerebral hemispheres that helps animals to adapt to their constantly changing environment.

Certain people seem to have an amazing sense of time—they can accurately name the hour of day and estimate time intervals and the duration of pauses. Since cosmonauts on an interplanetary flight will be living in a constant condition without geophysical factors such as night and day, and the seasons, what will happen to their physiological rhythm, their biological time?

The question has been studied in isolation chambers where, as we have said, geophysical factors can be eliminated. V. I. Myasnikov once conducted an experiment in which the subject knew that the experiment was to last seven days but was given no watch or other means to mark the passage of the day. He was allowed to sleep, eat, do exercises whenever he wished, but time went slowly. After several days he had so lost all sense of time that he got ready to leave the isolation chamber 14 hours before the period was up.

In another experiment a group of people ˙stayed in a specially equipped bunker deep underground, cut off from all noise for 18 days. It was left completely up to the subjects when they did their eating, sleeping, and waking and their physiological reactions were registered electronically. After 18 days the subjects' sense of time was off by 32.5 hours, as if the days had been not 24 hours long, but nearly 26.

Some interesting data has come from French speleologists in their studies of caves. In 1962 Michel Siff spent two months in a deep cave, and from his report it is clear that in conditions of solitude and isolation from the outside world the sense of time disintegrates. After 1000 hours, more than 40 days, he thought only 25 days had passed. When the experiment was over and his friends came for him, Siff said, "Had I known the end was so near I would have eaten the rest of the tomatoes and fruit."

Three years later a team of eight Hungarians spent a month in one of the caves in the Buda hills. The team had no watches or radios and when they received the order to come up to the surface they were four days behind. For the first ten days they had been well "synchronized" to actual time.

There have been other interesting experiments with "compressed" and "expanded" time. A group of subjects were given watches set, without their knowledge, to run fast or slow, and sent from England to Spitsbergen where in summer the Sun never sets. Although living in an isolated colony, the members of the team managed to lead comparatively normal lives, according to their incorrect watches. Because they were gaining or losing three hours a day (the changes went unnoticed) the actual weeks of the experiment were seven for those on a 21-hour day but only five for those on a 27-hour day. Thus time was either "expanded" or "compressed."

Similar experiments have been conducted in isolation chambers. Subject G. never noticed that his watch was losing 180 minutes a day, creating a 27-hour day. After 15 days he could not understand why the experiment had ended two days early.

So although physiological processes maintain a circadian rhythm under constant conditions, man cannot get along without his "timekeepers." It would seem wise to keep the space team on a long interplanetary flight on a normal daily regime. But this in all probability will not be possible.

The main function of man in the man-machine combination is to monitor the instruments. How long can the cosmonaut work up to capacity while on watch duty? In other words, how long before fatigue sets in and affects the quality of his work? We do not have a final answer, but using the facts gathered by physiologists and psychologists we are now trying to set the optimum watch period.

There is much evidence to the effect that after five or six hours, even with all automatic systems working uninterruptedly, a man gradually lets down his guard and becomes a less reliable link in the man-machine system. He tires more quickly if his emotions are negative for some reason.

If you consider the effect of all the unfavorable factors, including the long duration of the flight, then watch fatigue on the flights of the future will probably set in even earlier than five to six hours. On the basis of long atomic-submarine experience the optimal watch period, preceded by sleep, should probably not exceed four hours. The teams of the first interplanetary flights will be limited in number, making a four-hour watch shift difficult if not impossible to set up. Would it be possible then to alter the length of the day?

Studies of subway workers who have worked the night shift for years show that despite the long years of exclusively night duty, physiological rhythm, almost without exception, has not changed. Studies of railroad workers on freight trains whose days are often broken into irregular shifts of sleep and work show that over the course of the years the organism adapts to an unusual way of life. These people can fall asleep at any hour of the day even when daytime sleep during a long stopover has been preceded by a night's sleep at home. However, though they can adapt themselves to their regime, the normal daily fluctuation pattern of their physiological functions does not change.

It is interesting to observe those who must fly to other parts of the Earth where the time is different by 6 to 12 hours. Affected by the changed rhythm of geophysical factors and of human life around them, people become acclimatized within a matter of days (usually not more than 15), and the physiological processes shift to correspond to the new life conditions.

The pattern of physiological rhythm in plants and animals basically depends on light and temperature. The organism is an open system constantly under the influences of the atmosphere and constantly adapting itself to change. Such factors as light and temperature serve as signals to synchronize physiological functions with astronomical time.

Experiments studying the effect of various regimes on daily activity in conditions similar to those in space show that the greater the deviation from the normal regime the harder it is on the subject. Generally, after two to five days the cosmonauts work up to capacity again and sleep according to the new schedule. But a corresponding adaptation of pulse, respiration rate, and body temperature comes only after 8 to 15 days. The subjects continue to count time in terms of normal days and it is particularly hard on those who try to imagine what is going on outside the isolation chamber at any given time. In all probability in interplanetary flight time will have to be counted in terms of spacecraft time as opposed to Earth time, just as people think in terms of local time as opposed to time in some distant place.

For each interplanetary flight the daily regime will have to be set according to the number on the team, the amount of work to be done, and the space provided for leisure. It is conceivable that a "day" in space will be divided approximately like this: four hours of work, four of leisure, and four of sleep. But to avoid mental exhaustion work and leisure hours must be divided into various activities. Leisure hours will not be devoted exclusively to physical training. Work hours will not be just watch duty, but also experimental work. Creative work, of which we will speak later, will be enormously important in avoiding sensory starvation.

As a result of the intense work of the brain during waking hours and its constant responses to the stimuli from the outside world, we know that the brain cells become exhausted and must be restored to capacity by sleep. On an interplanetary flight it will be essential to provide conditions ensuring sleep for the cosmonauts.

On the eight-day American Gemini-5 flight sleeping shifts in working quarters proved difficult. Astronauts Cooper and Conrad complained that in the silence that reigned in the cabin, the slightest sound, even the pages of the flight log being turned, woke them up. On an interplanetary flight special living quarters will undoubtedly be necessary. If noise were to penetrate there, it might be possible to set up some kind of a monotonous background noise, like the surf or rain and wind, that would drown out the unwanted noise and encourage sleep. But cosmonauts will also have to develop their ability to fall asleep quickly whenever necessary.

Studies have shown that a four-hour sleep after an eight-hour waking period will fully restore a man to working capacity if each member of the space team adheres strictly to the set schedule of watch, leisure, and sleep. Further experiments on Earth and on orbital flights will undoubtedly establish the optimal daily rhythm for life in space more precisely.

The awakening of talent

Many of the psychic problems in isolation have developed in those who had no way to occupy their hours, no regimented program. In the battle against sensory starvation and sensory deception and boredom on a long space flight, the cosmonaut must learn how to spend his time in an interesting way.

As we said, during the experiments in isolation chambers the cosmonauts were given a program of activities that took up four hours of the day. The rest of the time they had to themselves. The first cosmonauts, Gagarin, Titov, Nikolaev, and Popovich, were allowed to read; others were not. Instead they were given colored pencils, paper, wood blocks, and knives and told to find their own ways to spend their free time.

During free time in the first few days they acquainted themselves with the isolation chamber, studied their instructions, and sometimes just sat doing nothing. On the second or third day the majority of them bestirred themselves to activity, and not without enthusiasm. Earlier they had tended to return to work ahead of time, but now, having found something interesting to do during their free time, they had some difficulty tearing themselves away.

Their activities varied, according to individual propensities. Titov recited the verse of his favorite poets aloud, Popovich sang Ukrainian songs. Some of them used wood and things like paper napkins and cotton wadding to make models and toys, some wrote poems and stories. Here is an example:

Tale from an Isolation Chamber

This is not a trip. I'd rather call it an adventure. My notes won't be as interesting or absorbing as Stefan Zweig's *Magellan* or *Thirty Years among the Indians*, but you may be curious about the world of the isolation chamber and the emotions of a man in one. Not a hero, just a man like yourself.

I'm writing these lines at the end of the fourth day in an isolation chamber. It's possible the story would be more beautiful if I wrote it afterward, sitting at my desk at home. But I'm afraid I'll forget, afraid of distorting the reality.

Before coming here I thought a lot about this great test. I was pretty familiar with the regime in an isolation chamber. You can live by one of two schedules. The first corresponds to astronomical time, the second reverses it: when it's daytime in the outside world, it is night in the isolation chamber.

I admit I didn't much want to live on reversed time. It's an additional hardship. I've had a lot of trouble in my life recently and I hoped the doctors would be humane.

Then it was the last interview and the chief medic Oleg Nikolaevich told me in no uncertain terms, "We're not running a spa here, you're going on reverse time." The decision was final and I didn't want to appeal it.

I packed my things: my gym suit, slide rule, pad of paper, pencils, and toothpaste. I'd be washing with cotton dipped in rose water, and cleaning my teeth with my tongue.

I took one "contraband" item: several dandelions which I picked just before going to the chamber. I just needed to take a little bit of spring with me. Oleg Nikolaevich saw my bouquet and said nothing. I don't know what his considerations were.

I was touched when they asked me what kind of concert I'd like for the day I leave the chamber. I asked for Mephistopheles' song and Figaro as sung by Muslim Magomaev, Prince Igor's aria, any recording by Edith Piaf.

Another cosmonaut tried his hand at verse:

Then We Are Going to Live

All right, this is isolation
From Earth, no communication
      But I have this to give:
      We are going to live
      When we get back from Mars.
      Having sowed seeds from Earth
      Man will have advanced and know the worth.

No guesswork about it
There'll be gardens on Mars all right
And we cosmonauts will sing in delight
      We can do it, it's ours to give
      And then we are going to live.

Our neighbor the Moon
Will reveal all its wonders
Its wind and rain and rivers
      Don't just sit there, I mean you
      There's work to be done

> To make the dream come true
> There is much you can give
> And then we are going to live.

On coming out of the isolation chamber many cosmonauts admitted they had never suspected themselves of having any creative interests or abilities before the test in the chamber.

There is another interesting way to pass the time. The French psychologist Paul Abeli has studied the psychology of the game played against oneself (a crossword, a rebus, a chess problem) and given it the name "ludism." Ludism differs from competitive games in that the effort and skill of the player are directed not against another person but himself. In conditions of prolonged solitude and extensive free time, ludism will be a salvation from boredom and exhausting inactivity.

"A man is judged," wrote Lenin, "not by what he says and thinks, but by his actions." A man's actions are the basic criterion for judging his thought and psychological capacities. That the creative efforts of the cosmonauts written in isolation were concerned not so much with self as with others has a profound social explanation—the collectivism typical of people in Soviet society.

And so we have come to the end of our story. We would like to remind the reader once more of the rigors of this profession that distinguish it from other human activities: the painstaking preparations for an encounter with the elements, the instantaneously fatal vacuum, the dangers of radiation and meteorite particles, repeated acceleration stress, the silence of the universe, the prolonged weightlessness, and many other factors, any one of which could be destructive and together might be much more dangerous.

The conquest of space is serious business and only possible for a society at a high level of accomplishment in science and technology; the cosmonaut must be able to keep up with all its accomplishments. He must know much and be capable of much. He must know the latest discoveries, everything that is going on in the laboratories, factories, engineering and research institutes. Such comprehensive knowledge is not easy in our day. The cosmonaut must learn mathematics, physics, astronomy, cybernetics, radio technology, electronics, metallurgy, chemistry, biology, psychology, physiology. To bear such a load one has to be in excellent health. Only a physically strong organism can sustain the training program. Only someone with a well-trained body, strong nerves, and stable psyche can successfully pass all the tests put to the man who has decided to become a cosmonaut. But physical stamina and outstanding skills are still not enough. There has to be persistence, determination, and selfless devotion to the goal. It is these that will help the highly educated and physically strong to conquer space, for space will submit only to the strong.